Frame by Frame

A VISUAL GUIDE TO COLLEGE SUCCESS

Sharyn Lowenstein, Ed.D
Bunker Hill Community College

Peaco Todd, M.A.
Lesley College

Cartoons by Peaco Todd

Prentice Hall
Upper Saddle River, NJ 07458

Library of Congress Cataloging–in–Publication Data

Todd, Peaco
    Frame by Frame : a visual guide to college success / Peaco Todd,
Sharyn Lowenstein.
       p. cm.
    Includes bibliographical references and index.
    ISBN 0-13-891268-8
    1. College student orientation   2. Study skills.   3. Caricatures,
and cartoons.   I. Lowenstein, Sharyn.   II. Title.
LB2343.3.T63   1999
                                    99-21376
                                       CIP

Production Editor: *Eileen M. O'Sullivan*
Managing Editor: *Mary Carnis*
Acquisitions Editor: *Sue Bierman*
Page Layout: *Stephen Hartner*
Director of Manufacturing and Production: *Bruce Johnson*
Cover and Interior Design: *Laura Ierardi*
Production Manager: *Marc Bove*
Marketing Manager: *Jeff McIlroy*
Editorial Assistant: *Amy Diehl*
Cover Artist: *Peaco Todd*
Creative Designer: *Marianne Frasco*
Cartoons: *Peaco Todd*
Printer/Binder: *Banta Digital Group*

©1999 by Prentice-Hall, Inc.
Simon & Schuster / A Viacom Company
Upper Saddle River, New Jersey 07458

Printed in the United States of America

10 9 8 7 6 5 4 3 2 1

ISBN 0-13-891268-8

Prentice-Hall International (UK) Limited, *London*
Prentice-Hall of Australia Pty. Limited, *Sydney*
Prentice-Hall Canada Inc., *Toronto*
Prentice-Hall Hispanoamericana, S.A., *Mexico*
Prentice-Hall of India Private Limited, *New Delhi*
Prentice-Hall of Japan, Inc., *Tokyo*
Simon & Schuster Asia Pte. Ltd., *Singapore*
Editora Prentice-Hall do Brasil, Ltda., *Rio de Janeiro*

Dedicated to:

Eddie Lowenstein
who taught me to respect words,
and Lois Spiegleman,
who inspired me to play with them.

My father, Peaco Todd,
who taught me that life is shaped by small joys,
and Brad,
who shows me every day that laughter is the greatest gift of all.

Contents

x

Preface

The authors, Sharyn Lowenstein and Peaco Todd, participated in a brief interview about *Frame by Frame*.

• Why did you decide to write Frame by Frame?

SL: I've always wanted to write an academic book. One day about four years ago I read a humorous academic piece by a colleague. Somehow that triggered the realization that I could write a study skills book which was whimsical, offbeat, upbeat and substantive without being overwhelming. When I saw Peaco's delightful cartooning I thought this is the perfect partnership. I would bring my knowledge and experience as an educator working with students around issues in study skills, college adjustment, learning styles, disabilities, and communication, and Peaco would bring her knowledge of cartooning and graphic design, and her experience as a writer and educator.

• How did you develop the cartoon characters?

PT: Sharyn and I agreed from the beginning that we wanted the characters to represent a diverse group, not just of gender and race, but also of learners. Every one approaches college, social life, friends, romance, and their dreams of the future in very different ways, and we all have the potential to be successful. When I first began developing the characters, I really didn't know how they would come out, or even really who they were. I just tried to begin drawing a range of character types in various situations. But almost immediately, their distinct personalities began to emerge, and very quickly they came alive. They began telling me what they wanted to say, and showing me how they would behave. Now I see them as characters who have lives and spirits of their own. For me, this is the best part of being a car-toonist: when the characters I think I'm creating and controlling end up surprising and teaching me.

• What was one of your high points in creating this book?

SL: One of the high points for me was seeing the cartoons in full color. They were more vibrant than I could have imagined. And somehow – I don't know why this is true – but the color, the shading, and the texture, gave an immediacy to the characters and situations and made them even more compelling and comprehen-sive. Getting feedback from others was also a high point. It's wonderful to know that the vision you had actually comes through in the final product.

PT: For me, I think it was the first time I really could see it coming together, when I could see how the cartoons fit so beautifully with the text, and how well they worked to inform and enhance each other.

• *What's the best way to read Frame by Frame?*

PT: I would say, whatever fits your style will suit this book. If you like to skip around, or read those sections first that are of greater interest, that's fine.

SL: In fact, we encourage readers to play with the sequence. Some sections will be fun at first, but make a lot more sense after you've given them some thought and come back to them later. Many sections build on others. Time management, for example, is not only addressed in Chapter Four but in Chapter Seven and lots of other places. Dealing with relationships is addressed in almost every cartoon. Stress management is addressed in Chapter Twelve, but also starts building in Chapters Two and Three. Many of the cartoons, which we hope are ideal for their sections, also work for other sections as well. So, if readers are willing to play with the text, and experiment with the way they read, they will find new connections across and within the chapters. I would also say that no matter how students read the text, starting with *Meet the Cast* will introduce them to the characters quickly and make the whole book more enjoyable.

PT: The cartoon/text "mix" is an interesting one: Each chapter section is really inseparable from its cartoon, but the cartoons also can be read independently. If you look at them from front to back, they do tell a kind of story, but each one also works alone.

SL: The cartoons are intended to develop points from the text or introduce some of the ideas in the text. And the text is intended to enhance the cartoons.

• *What do you want students to get out of this book?*

SL: I'd really like for readers to believe in themselves and their ability, to use their sense of humor to laugh at and with the characters and at the situations academic life can bring. I hope that readers will be encouraged by the strong themes of self-advocacy and trial and error that run though the text, and that they will be open to taking risks so that they get what they need to learn. I hope *Frame by Frame* encourages readers to recognize and celebrate their successes. This may sound corny, but I want students to find their own study muses, because there really is an Angela in us all.

PT: I'd really like this book to say to students, "You don't have to be perfect. You don't have to know all the answers. College is a time to try new things, meet new people, and explore what you want to do and become. You have power, to learn what you need to succeed in school, and to begin the journey that has already begun to unfold." And if *Frame by Frame* can help students realize that both work and dreams are best approached with a little laughter, then I will consider the book a success.

Acknowledgments

First we thank our main cast – Shalimar, Amy, Skip, Nathan, Phyllis (and, of course Reba), Chen, Angela and Armande – you have been living in our heads and hearts! You've inspired us throughout the writing of Frame by Frame.

Thank you, Karen Austin, for your enthusiastic response to our early ideas and for introducing us to the other staff at Prentice Hall. Many thanks to our editor, Todd Rossell, who took a chance on the unusual concept of this book; Amy Diehl, who helped us navigate the complicated publishing arena; and Mary Carnis and Eileen O'Sullivan, who have been instrumental in laying out the format, which turned out to be no easy task!

We are indebted to all of our colleagues who have supported this project. To Laura Kranis, you always responded to our SOS calls and provided more insightful feedback than you can ever imagine. To Jean Zipke, Margaret Pobywajlo, Cindy Gannett, Molly Finegan, Susan Huard, Pat Malinowski, Jackie Simons, Elisa Birdseye, Phil Tetreault, Wendela Yeo, and Barbara Gross, your support and thoughtful comments kept us going, and going, and going.

To colleagues at Bunker Hill Community College, Joanne Preston, Becky Briggs, Stephen Shore, Tusi Gastonguay, Bill McCarthy, Sara Satham, Margaret Suby, Eileen Berger, Jean Bernard, Jackie Kiddy, and Diane Smith, your help in reading the manuscript, providing references, and brainstorming ideas meant so much. To colleagues at Lesley College, and in particular Lynne Morrow: you gave the gift of time which allowed space for the book to unfold.

A special thanks to Deb Westaway, Duke Graham, Wayne Cormier, Eilene S. Shakespear, and Laura Kranis for class testing the book. To the students who participated in the class testing – Ellie Polin, Rafael Viera, Leah Blackstone, Mirko S. Chardin, Keisha Garcia, Lisa Faretra, G. Reyes, Eulises Cornejo, A. Gokboru, Jason Whitman, Robert Smart, and Randall Thomson, and many others – a heartfelt thanks.

And, finally to our families, your love and caring were essential. To John Bradley: you were a constant source of love, faith, and, most of all, humor throughout the long drawing days. To Mae Lowenstein, Dearest mom, your enthusiasm really helped! Thank you, thank you, Gregg Tolly, for living in book mania, for providing ongoing and loving technical assistance, and for steadfastly believing in this project.

About the Authors

Sharyn Lowenstein, Ed.D.

For over 20 years I have been an adult educator and teacher of undergraduate and graduate students, in degree and non-credit programs in community colleges, four-

year institutions, in public and private higher education. I have taught study skills, writing, and communication courses. I have also directed Learning Centers, trained tutors, and tutored students at all levels. I have particular interests in figuring out where learners are, and then organizing instruction and creating materials that work. I am also a quilter. I've come to realize that *Frame by Frame* is a text/pictorial quilt, whose pieces interact across chapters. Reading this quilt requires an ongoing partnership between us, the authors, in putting the project together, and you, the readers, in experimenting and playing with the words and images.

Peaco Todd, M.A.

Over the last four years, in addition to serving as an assistant professor at Lesley College in Cambridge, MA, I have published single-panel cartoons in a variety of

magazines as well as articles on subjects from Shakespeare to sailing (I once was part of a four-person crew delivering a trimaran from Spain to the Persian Gulf). In 1996 I illustrated *Talk It Out: Conflict Resolution in the Elementary Classroom*, by Barbara Porro (ASCD Books). I love noticing how seemingly disparate things relate to each other, and how these patterns can inspire images that have meaning and resonance. For me, this is also the stuff of humor: the unexpected connections that hide beneath the surface and startle us into laughing together. I invite you to visit my website at www.reuben.org/peaco.

1

Meet the Cast

You're about to begin a great adventure, and we'd like to offer some help and humor along the way.

The purpose of this chapter is for you to:

- Get acquainted with the cartoon cast of characters
- Become familiar with the tone and format of *Frame by Frame*
- Begin understanding the vocabulary and special features of the cartoons
- Feel encouraged to preview the topics covered in the rest of the book

● *Activity 1.1*

Survey your college campus. Find two places where you feel comfortable enough to study. Then write a brief description of these places by answering the following questions:

- Where are your special places?
- Why have you chosen these two spots?
- Which assignments might you tackle in each place?

● *Activity 1.2*

Look at the cartoon on the cover. The characters are responding to the news that they've been accepted into college. Each character has a different reaction, which tells us something about who they are, how they feel, and what they might expect.

Remember when you received your college acceptance, or, if your college had open admissions, recall when you received your first official letter after enrolling. Add a final frame to the cartoon with *you* in it. How are you responding to this news?

Even if you don't think you can draw, you can still do this or any other exercise in the book that asks you to add yourself as a cartoon character in the frame. Represent yourself with any sort of drawing you like, even a stick figure, a blob, or a circle face.

If you want to explore more fully how you can create and develop your own cartoon character, check out *"Draw Yourself In"* in Appendix 1.

2

The Show Begins

Any sort of change, especially a life-altering one like beginning college, brings its own special challenges. As you start, take some time to reflect on the "big picture" and begin to develop some strategies for managing your new circumstances.

The purpose of this chapter is for you to

- Develop an overall purpose for being in college
- Orient yourself in the first week of college
- Discover more about transitions and consider your current transitional stage
- Set up and maintain your personal study space
- Develop a workable set of goals regarding what you want to get from your college experiences
- Identify the significant parts of your life and become aware of the need to balance these parts

2.1 • Why You're in College

Here you are. You're starting college, maybe in a new town or unfamiliar part of the country. The expectations, challenges, and rewards of this new life are waiting for you. The clearer you are about why you're in college, the more successful you'll be. Below are some possible reasons:

Academic:

- Study _____ field
- Develop my skills in _____
- Develop myself intellectually

Job/Career:

- Get the credentials necessary to become a _____
- Make more money
- Get a promotion
- Decide on a career
- Position myself to compete better in the job market

Social:

- Make new friends
- Widen my networking circle
- Keep up with my friends who are in college

Personal:

- Become the best I can be
- Be a better parent for my child
- Set an example for my family
- Get away from home
- Find a place for myself in the world
- Meet my family's expectations that I go to college

Other:

- Improve my English language skills
- I didn't have a choice; it was always assumed
- My place of employment has a good tuition reimbursement policy
- Don't know what to do with my life; this seemed like a good way to find out

Once you've read the list of reasons

1. Rank your top three to five reasons.

2. Once you've selected your reasons, make them as specific as possible. (For example, if you'd like to study in the field of psychology, what aspects do you want to know more about? General psychology? The central nervous system? Psychological disorders?)

3. Find ways to explore each of your reasons further. Consider classes you could take and on- or off-campus activities you could attend that correspond to your interests. Have conversations with faculty, staff, or your peers who know about the areas in which you're interested.

4. If you don't really know why you're in college or you don't think your reasons for attending college are strong enough, seek out your advisor, talk to friends, or find a mentor. It's worth taking the time to find those reasons that really matter to you and make it all worthwhile.

5. Remember, once you've developed a list of three to five strong reasons for attending college, on a bad day you can use this page to remind yourself about what's keeping you in school. The stronger your reasons, the harder you'll try to do your best.

6. Don't be surprised if, over time, your reasons change. This shift is natural and just part of the college experience. So, why not return to this list of reasons each semester and rank-order them again?

2.2 • The Price of Admission: One Big Transition

Just in case you haven't noticed, you're in a transition: one of those challenging times in your life that requires new ways of thinking, solving problems, and reorganizing yourself. It could look this way: Last year you had free time, but now you have much less. Last year you had familiar tasks and responsibilities; now you have to learn a lot of new things. Last year you hung out with longtime friends, but this year you're surrounded by new faces. Maybe you've been through transitions before, but if not, you'll certainly be involved in some now.

Examples of transitions:

- Getting a new job/going into a new career
- Going into a relationship with a new partner
- Experiencing the death of a parent
- Separating/divorcing a spouse or splitting up with a partner
- Having a child
- Losing a friend
- Leaving home
- Losing a job
- Entering college

Transitions come in stages.

While each person's transition has its own individual course, there are some milestones along the way that many people experience. Read the stages below. Do any of these stages sound familiar?

Stage One: Are you numb? Perhaps you don't feel much of anything because you're in shock, overwhelmed, or paralyzed.

Stage Two: Are you denying or minimizing the impact of college? Even when others can see you're exhausted, are you taking on additional hours at work? Are you going to bed consistently late, even though you have very early morning classes?

Stage Three: Are you doubting yourself, feeling depressed or angry? Are your changes catching up with you? Maybe you're not sure you can handle the academic workload or the juggling of the academic work along with all your other responsibilities. Do you sometimes get angry—at yourself for not being more capable or working harder, at your teachers for not being more understanding, at the college for insisting that first-year students have a crazy schedule?

Stage Four: Are you at the point of letting go of the past and accepting your new status? Are you beginning to realize that you need to make some changes (in your study habits, how you spend your time, your relationships with old friends)? Have you come to the conclusion that while going to school is harder than you thought, it's also manageable?

Stage Five: Are you now trying out new habits? Some examples: You've bought your first big wall calendar; you go to the library, even though you haven't seen the inside of one for years; you discover that discussing your paper is a very good idea. You experience the joys of learning new skills and the frustrations when you don't learn them fast enough.

Transitions can affect your self-esteem because you can be so up and down emotionally. One minute you're confused, the next you've got it together. Today you're very happy with your choices, but tomorrow you may question them. You will get through it. Just don't beat yourself up if you can't figure it all out today! Eventually, you will start to make sense of this new stage in your life, feel confident about how college is turning out, and see that your journey is worthwhile.

 **HOT TIP!**   *If your transition is stressing you out, see Chapter 12.*

2.3 • Getting Oriented: What You Can Do in Your First Week

To launch yourself into the college environment, here are some things you can do during your first week.

Get a campus map (usually part of the course catalogue and often also a separate flyer) and give yourself a tour. Find these places:

- Locations of each of your classes and your advisor
- Campus bookstore
- Your student mailbox
- Student union and food areas
- Bank machines
- Telephones
- Library
- Computer labs
- Health services
- Sport or exercise center
- Counseling center
- Tutoring center
- Xeroxing places
- Faxing places
- Financial aid office/campus jobs postings
- Parking areas
- Good study areas

What else you can do in your first week:

- Buy your texts for each course.
- Get a student ID and a library card.
- Go through the student handbook and get familiar with your institution's rules.
- Get a course catalogue and become acquainted with:

    Your college's requirements for your major

    Courses you might like to take

    Graduation requirements

    Extracurricular activities

    The academic calendar and important dates

Befriend department secretaries

Secretaries (or administrative assistants) are some of the most valuable and overlooked resources on campus. They can tell you when your teacher (or the dean) will return and when he or she is likely to be most available and receptive. They can pass on notes or papers or tell you where to place notes or papers so they can be seen easily. For true emergencies, secretaries can sometimes fit you in for a quick appointment. (We don't recommend asking for this kind of special treatment on a frequent basis.) As in any other relationship, don't take secretaries for granted and always thank them for their information and help. (*Special hint:* Go out of your way to say hello on a day when you want absolutely no information or help from them.)

2.4 • Organizing and Maintaining Your Study Space

You know you'll create a study space, right? But where will it be and what will it include? Suppose you're already cramped. We still urge you to set up an area that's all yours. While you're at it, make it a place where you want to be, so you'll use it often. Remember, too, that setting up is only half the battle: The other half is keeping yourself organized so you're ready for college's little (and big) surprises.

Setting up your space:

- Take the time to plan where everything goes: Some arrangements will be much better for you than others.

- Decide where to place the phone. If you're easily distracted by phone calls, you might want it some distance away.

- Consider your physical position with regard to doors and windows. Will you be better focused if your view is of a wall or out of a window?

- Make sure you have enough light, a comfortable chair, and plenty of organizers, such as cans, crates, and boxes.

- Remember to create a space that is yourself-friendly. Include some personal mementos: photographs, posters, ticket stubs, programs, or other things that are meaningful to you.

Keeping yourself organized:

- Every one or two weeks put things in order.

- While you're straightening up, take 15 minutes to evaluate how well your space is working and make any changes necessary.

- Keep your supplies replenished. Running out of paper at 2 A.M. on the day your project is due can definitely cramp your style!

- Keep sorting and separating your supplies and notes so you can easily find them.

Expanding your space if you need more:

- Install shelves to make use of wall space.

- Check to see if your closet could hold your dresser or filing cabinet.

- Look for ways to maximize your drawer space (for example, drawer organizers) or add shelves to closets and wall cabinets.

- Put a door or board over filing cabinets to make a desk or storage shelf.

- If space is especially tight, consider building a hinged shelf to use as a writing space or put your mattress on a high platform and build a study space under the loft.

Checklist of some essential study items

Dictionary	Lined notebooks and pads
Thesaurus	Post-it® notes
Pencils and pencil sharpener	Three-ring notebooks and three-ring manila pockets
Pens and highlighters	Wall calendar
Computer and printer	Pocket diary or planner with schedule
Writing and computer paper	Mini tape recorder and tapes
Back-up disks	Paper clips, stapler, and staples
Calculator	Ear plugs
File folders and file box	Clock

2.5 • Setting Goals

For your college journey, plan goals that will help you end up where you want to be and give you some interesting experiences along the way.

Create goals that work for you:

- Write your goals down. Include big, far-reaching goals as well as smaller, more incremental milestones.

- Read over your goals frequently. If a goal no longer seems important, don't hesitate to write a new one.

- Phrase your goals so that you can actually measure your progress. "Become a famous writer" is both big and pretty vague. Make it more specific, such as "This year complete and submit one piece to the campus literary magazine."

- Focus your goals on your own will and ability: Don't make your goals dependent upon other people. You cannot control what others will do, but you can take charge of your own actions.

- Notice when you reach the small and big goals. Celebrate your successes.

Try this exercise

Write about your goals as if they were accomplished. Add five years to the current date. Then write a page or two about your life, in the present tense, as if you had achieved everything on your list of goals. If, for example, two of your goals are to become a successful environmental lawyer and live by the ocean, you might write, "I'm sitting on my redwood deck watching the sun set over the Pacific Ocean and reading a newspaper article about how I won an injunction against the clearcutting of California redwoods. On the table next to me is a key to my new corner office on the 35th floor at Dorke & Nerrd. I am the youngest person ever to become a partner…" You get the idea.

2.6 • Fitting the Pieces Together

Your life is a thousand-piece jigsaw puzzle. The pieces are your school, work, family, social, and personal activities.

Don't construct your puzzle with only complicated pieces:

- To the extent that you are able, choose pieces that work well together. If you have a heavy semester (and the first semester is almost always heavy), try to find work or an internship that is less stressful, at hours best for your schedule and in places that don't require long commutes. Don't fool yourself into thinking that it will all fall smoothly into place. Keep remembering that the first year at college is an especially big adjustment.

- If it makes sense, consider on-campus work or internship placements. Supervisors in academic institutions tend to be understanding of your school-related juggling and will sometimes allow you to adjust your schedule during crunch times. Check your financial aid office, human resources office (for work opportunities), and academic departments (for internship possibilities).

Communicate clearly:

- Let the people you live with know your schedule and how you can be reached. Make sure you know how to reach them.

- Before committing to work or an internship, make sure you understand the expectations of both the company (or agency) and your supervisor.

- If you are already employed, before you commit to school (or change your school schedule) you might want to talk over your situation with your immediate supervisor. Find ways to make your new arrangements satisfying to you both. Once you've reached an understanding, write your supervisor a brief note that summarizes your agreement. Keep a copy for yourself.

- If your work supervisor suddenly needs more of your time or starts giving you more responsibility or things to learn, consider your options. Discuss the situation with her and see if there's any room for adjustment.

- If you have a job/internship that requires missing even 15 minutes from a class on a regular basis, discuss this situation with your professor. Make sure to work out a satisfactory arrangement. For example, maybe another student could lend you her notes.

- If there's a work-related trip or event that will interfere with a class, approach your professor as soon as you know. Do not assume your professor will automatically be pleased. Check the attendance policy before you approach your professor and work out a way to make up missed assignments and lost class time.

- Sometimes making even a slight schedule adjustment can help immensely. For example, use part of a lunch or dinner hour at your internship or work site to do some studying.

Fitting all the pieces together is an ongoing process. And once you've got the pieces more or less in place, keep checking to make sure no one area of your life is suffering. Try asking yourself these questions, and make adjustments accordingly.

- Am I getting all my assignments in on time?
- Am I running late more often than I'd like?
- Am I skipping meals or eating too much fast food?
- Am I skimping on my coursework, my job or internship, my family time?
- Have I communicated clearly with my professors and supervisors?
- Are there other adjustments I still need to make?

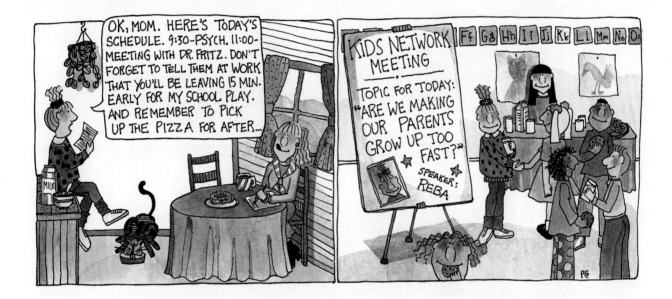

2.7 • The Balancing Act

Imagine that college is like riding a skateboard: In order to go forward you have to constantly adjust your weight as you're pushed and pulled. As your own needs and pressures change, you'll want to re-evaluate the balance of activities and responsibilities in your life, and make adjustments.

● *Activity 2.1*

Locate two places on campus where you think you'll feel comfortable studying. Describe these places and explore how they will provide a good study environment for you.

● *Activity 2.2*

Look at the cartoon frames in "The Price of Admission: One Big Transition." Of the reactions given, which one feels closest to yours? If you can't find one that fits, create a frame in which you present your own character. Write a caption for your character.

3

Learning How You Learn

On this journey, your unique strengths, challenges, and circumstances will play significant roles in your success. College is about learning, but it's also about getting to know yourself in a different light.

The purpose of this chapter is for you to:

- Determine your strengths as a learner
- Discover your challenges as a learner
- Become more skilled in working with any disabilities you may have
- More effectively meet your needs if you are an international student
- Figure out how to make your life experiences and daily rhythms work for you
- Start taking advantage of services, resources, and extracurricular options

3.1 • Working with Your Strengths

Start with your strengths. Get to know them, use them, play with them, experiment. Don't discount your strengths in areas that might seem unrelated to academics—athletics, dancing, coaching, music, working with tools, and other hobbies or interests. You just have to figure out a way to use them. And don't forget: Strengths aren't just those abilities that come easily to you. You can develop strengths in areas that now challenge you.

How to discover your strengths:

- Understand that strengths come in four areas: what you can do, what you know, what your attitudes are, and what your values are. Most likely you have many strengths in each of these areas.

- Remember a time when you were really pleased with yourself. Maybe it was how you acted or something you accomplished. Did you persist when a situation seemed hopeless? Did you contribute to a group effort or team?

- Think about two or three things that felt difficult or "unnatural" that you still learned how to do. Maybe you're incredibly disorganized, but you made yourself devise and then stick to a system for keeping things in order. Even if it isn't easily accessible, whatever quality emerged is still a part of you and can be tapped into again.

- Make a personal inventory. Write down the activities you like to do and the things you're good at doing (not necessarily the same). This is not a time for humility! Include something from each area of your life: academic, social, family, clubs, and hobbies. Then examine the list and identify all your strengths—skills, knowledge areas, attitudes, and values.

How to work with your strengths:

Practice:

- Remember to use your strengths, or they'll get rusty.

Apply your strengths to new contexts:

- Use a strength in a new setting. For example, say you're really good at getting people talking in social situations. This set of skills can be extremely useful in certain kinds of research.

Put yourself in settings that agree with you:

- Choose environments that nourish your strengths. Whenever possible, surround yourself with people who encourage your growth.

- Be receptive to situations that require learning a new skill or "massaging" an existing one. (For example, you're writing a research paper, but you feel it's dull. You apply your storytelling skills to create an interesting opening scene that grabs your audience.)

How to grow a strength from a weakness:

The Blueprint:

Often, weaknesses turn into strengths because you're inspired by something you really want or need to do. Both motivations work!

1. Look at your objective. What would it require in terms of time, skill, knowledge, and money? It might mean some big changes in your life: Is it worth it? For example, if you are a novice but want to become an expert skier, are you willing to spend the time necessary to learn this complex skill? Can you take on the large expense of equipment and lift tickets?

2. Figure out the parts you already do well or have in place. Also, look at what you will need to do and what weaknesses you will need to address. If you dream of becoming an acupuncturist, but struggle with reading the technical material required for certification, you might take reading classes, work with a tutor, or learn to take notes in a way that helps you understand them.

3. Work on those weak areas, one at a time. Make a plan, practice the skill, get feedback on how you're doing, find ways to learn how to do it better, and give yourself rewards.

3.2 • The Million Dollar Learning Style

There's one learning style that's priceless. Once discovered, it will help you study the most difficult material, navigate the toughest course, understand the hardest professor, and make the most efficient use of your time and energy. This priceless learning style is…your own. It's the unique approach you use—all the methods and adaptations you make—to get the most out of each learning situation. It pays to discover how you learn.

Observe:

With so much to learn in college, you have many opportunities to find out what approaches work the best for you. Take an active interest in how you learn by observing yourself as you take in information.

Keep track:

Figure out how you're attempting to learn material and the extent to which your methods are working. For example, to memorize many facts for your history course, you copied the facts longhand, repeated them out loud, and drew a chart of the facts. All three methods seemed to be helpful, but you think the chart is the most effective.

Keep asking yourself questions:

1. Looking back on my school career, what three to five classes have been my favorites? What three to five classes have been my least favorites? Why?

2. Which of my current classes is my least favorite? Why?

3. If I had to describe one moment in each of my classes in which everything was very clear and I was learning something, what would it be? Why?

4. In social situations, when am I most comfortable and when am I least comfortable? (Do I find myself talking to lots of people altogether? One person at time? Am I mostly a "people watcher"?)

5. What is the easiest way for me to follow directions? (Write them down? Hear them? Get in the car and find my own way? See a map? Some combination?)

6. How do I learn best when doing other things, such as fixing my car, playing an instrument, or learning a new skill at a job?

7. Which of my texts is most readable? What techniques draw my interest or make the material accessible? (Wide margins? Lots of examples? Charts? Personal tone? Lists? Short paragraphs? Sidebars? Questions?)

Work with what you now know about yourself:

Using the information you've gathered from the previous questions, and also from what you've already noticed about yourself, think about how you learn best. Perhaps you think of yourself as someone who needs to "see" things in order to understand them (a visual learner). Maybe it is easier for you to hear information than to see it (an auditory learner). Or, maybe you like to discover something by doing it. Perhaps you need a combination of techniques.

However, try to avoid labeling yourself. Just because you're more of a visual learner, for example, doesn't mean that any visual approach will work for you: A demonstration might be more effective for you than seeing those same steps illustrated on a page. You constantly have to tailor an approach to what you're trying to learn.

Experiment, tinker, and play:

Experiment with the many different methods you can try. For example, if you think you learn best by hearing information, you could tape selected parts of classes or read your notes or papers out loud. If one method isn't right for you, keep adjusting it. You can even create something new.

Tinker with small variations in a technique and notice how these variations affect your learning. For example, instead of just highlighting your text, use colored stars in the margins to indicate important points.

Play with the combination of methods as well as the order of techniques you try. For example, you might get the most out of a lecture class by taking notes, reciting them out loud, and then discussing the class session with a friend. Another student might try the same combination of methods, but prefer to discuss the lecture before copying over his notes.

Hey, it's Mr. Question-Person *!*

Each week Mr. Question-Person roams the campus armed with only a notebook and camera, seeking answers to today's hard student questions. He strikes without warning, so watch out: maybe this week you'll find yourself in Mr. Question-Person!

This week's question: Do You Have An Alternative Learning Style?

Naila B.
Major:
Agronomy

"**I learn best in groups:** the cross-pollination of ideas and the growth of knowledge. Maybe it's not traditional, but now it's mainstream!"

Tab H.
Major:
Undeclared

"I haven't decided. I'm still exploring my options. There are so many ways to go. Next semester I'll have one."

Nathan J.
Major:
Computer
Science

"I have several alternatives. I can use either logic or analysis or computation. I think, therefore I learn!"

Gabriella M.
Major:
Fashion
Design

"I'm always coming up with new styles. This semester I'm really into visuals. I think it's setting a trend."

3.3 • Working with Your Learning Challenges

The good news about learning challenges is that whatever yours happen to be, you're not alone. The truth of the matter is that we all have learning challenges. As you stretch yourself in college and try to take in more information, learn new skills, meet new people, and in general more fully develop yourself, you'll probably run up against areas that are more tricky for you, that require much more effort than others. It's natural to want to avoid your challenge areas. Resist this temptation, and you'll become a much stronger learner.

In academic life learning challenges can affect how you listen, read, organize your work, write, speak out in class, make presentations, participate in class discussions, relate to your faculty, and take exams. Even with exactly the same type of learning challenge, no two people have the same experience.

Consider this: Whatever your courseload, there is actually an additional hidden class you are taking. You haven't officially registered for it, but it's an essential part of your college career. This class is your very own "lab" course, the one you are in every day, with every assignment. In your personal lab you are discovering your learning challenges—experimenting, noting your progress, and figuring out ways to survive, and even thrive, in each of your other courses.

Some Academic Learning Challenges

Challenge	Examples
Reading Pronunciation	• You might delete whole lines, words, or word endings. You might reverse letters or insert them where they don't belong.
Reading Comprehension	• You might be good at finding facts but have real difficulty understanding how these facts add up to something bigger. Maybe you can't seem to find the main point, or you do but then later you can't remember the material.
Writing	• You might have difficulty writing sentences without omitting words or parts of words. Or you just can't seem to develop your ideas enough to please your teachers.
Discussion	• You get lost. By the time you figure out who's speaking, the speaker has changed.
Spatial	• You go left when you want to go right, have trouble following maps, travel directions, graphs. You have trouble reading shapes. Tests with matching questions are particularly difficult.
Social	• Your social timing is a bit off. You ask questions when you should be listening. You don't seem to know what to do in social situations. You've been told you don't know how to "read" people, or you avoid them because it's easier than interacting.
Attention	• Perhaps you have a tendency to do things or blurt things out without thinking them through; your mind wanders; you're involved in many activities without finishing any; you have difficulty starting something, or if you start, you have difficulty staying with it; you have a constant need to keep moving and an extreme sensitivity to sights and sounds.
Mathematics	• Perhaps you have trouble computing, following steps, or working a problem through to the end.

3.4 • If You Are a Student with Disabilities

If you have a disability, it may be possible to get adjustments or accommodations made, depending on the nature of your disability. Sometimes students decline adjustments because they don't want special treatment. It's better to think of accommodations as interventions that make it possible for you to do your best work while still meeting faculty standards. Accommodations can make a huge difference in helping you stay in school and do well. You have a legal right to them, as spelled out in federal legislation—the 1990 Americans with Disabilities Act and Section 504 of the Rehabilitation Act of 1973[1].

Documentation:

In most instances, especially with learning disabilities, in order to show you have a disability you'll need to furnish documentation, papers that show you have been tested by a certified professional in the field. This documentation should describe the disability in a way that is comprehensible to others and provide recommendations of accommodations that can or should be made and the circumstances under which you should be accommodated. Documentation less than three years old is generally accepted; some schools may be more fussy than others about how recent the documentation must be.

Sharing information about your disability:

If you want to get accommodations, you will need to share information not only about the nature of your disability but also about how it affects your learning and the way you show what you have learned (for example, how you test or contribute to class discussions). The question about how much to share is a very personal decision. You will probably want to discuss your decision with a knowledgeable person you trust. You should also clarify who has access to your documents and where they will be filed. Some people think a good plan is to tell only what others need to know to help you learn best. Most likely, the first person you'll share your documentation with is a counselor from the Office of Student Disabilities (or whatever the equivalent is in your school). Once you meet, you'll put together a plan for each semester that includes your accommodations and other services that will support you.

Accommodations:

There is a variety of accommodations possible. The accommodations should match the documentation and be appropriate for each student in each situation; the accommodations must provide what the student needs and no more. A student may need an accommodation in one class, but not in another. An accommodation needed at first may be unnecessary later. Some of the more common accommodations include testing and other work adjustments:

- More time (time and a half or double time is frequent) for tests and projects
- An alternative testing space that has minimal or no distractions
- An alternate test form (for example, an oral exam rather than a written exam; use of a computer or spellchecker during tests)

- Relocation of a class to accommodate physical disabilities
- Use of taped books, articles, and handouts through Recordings for the Blind, a Kurzweil machine, or voice-activated software
- Use of a notetaker or reader
- Tutoring (or, if there is a tutoring quota, permission to exceed that limit when needed)
- Permission to tape record your classes

Your responsibility

As with any right (in this case, to pursue reasonable accommodations), you also have responsibilities.

Know what your disability is and be able to describe it so other people can understand it. It's extremely helpful if you not only name it, but can also discuss what it means for you. For example, if you have a reading disability, be able to explain how long it takes you to read a page or a chapter and how much of the material you are able to remember afterwards. Be positive in your explanation, rather than demanding or complaining.

Consult your student handbook, course catalogue, and other school publications so you know your school's guidelines and where to go for information and support.

Register with the appropriate office if you decide to share this information.

Once you make the decision to share this information, tell your professor as early as possible, so that together you can plan appropriately. Waiting until a few days before an exam (or, worse, after an exam) to ask for extended time might result in your not getting the accommodation

Understand that you are your own best advocate, no matter how organized or dedicated the Office of Student Disabilities may be. Realize that you may be your professor's main source of information on your type of disability.

Get your course books as early as possible. Work with the bookstore, professors, the library, student affairs, and the Office of Student Disabilities.

3.5 • Know Your Daily Rhythms

We all have a natural rhythm for doing our best work. Exploring when you're at your peak will help you create an effective study schedule.

Questions about daily rhythms:

- Are you naturally an early riser, or is it a struggle to get out of bed for morning classes?

- What do you consider an early class? A late class?

- What times of the day do you usually feel most alert, enthusiastic, and creative?

- What times of day do you feel less energetic, or more tired and cranky?

- What's your favorite time of day?

- What time of the day do you do your fun activities?

- If you could add an hour to the day, where would you put it?

Other things to think about:

- Besides daily cycles, we also have cycles over the course of a week, and a month (yes, guys, even you).

- Some people have strong reactions either to the beginning or the end of the week.

- Seasons matter, too. Some people get more tired and depressed when there's less light.

Try identifying those tasks that don't require much energy and do these when you're less alert. If you think you're more of a morning person, try giving yourself as much time to do the hard stuff in the morning. If you have morning classes, it may mean going to sleep a bit earlier so that you can get up earlier to work. Create a fantasy schedule. See when you would do things if you could. Then try to make your real schedule more like your ideal one.

3.6 • One Person's Music Is Another Person's Noise

Have you ever been so distracted by a noise that you couldn't think? Or found that you just had to have certain sounds in your environment in order to be able to concentrate? As you tackle complex material in college, it will become even more essential that you create the best study environment for yourself. Deciding what auditory environment you need, what you can't tolerate, and what other people want and desire is all part of learning. People vary tremendously. One person's music is another person's noise.

Here are just a few examples of how different we are:

- For some, noise interference is any music; for others it might be, say, just country/western.

- For some, soft background sounds are essential; for others these are a maddening distraction and only total silence will work.

- For some, the sounds of many simultaneous conversations are fine; for others, even distant talking is bothersome.

- For some, TV is a temptation to avoid work and a huge time waster; for others, background TV helps facilitate certain kinds of repetitive or less challenging homework.

A few potential solutions to noise interference:

- Block sounds out by using ear plugs and white noise gadgets such as fans and humidifiers.

- Control your environment: Use earphones, find a place to study that has the kind of sound (or quiet) you want, negotiate the amount and type of sound with roommates and/or family.

If you live in close proximity to someone whose auditory needs differ from yours, you probably will have to negotiate some compromises. This requires sensitivity, flexibility, and the willingness to keep talking about these issues and making adjustments.

When negotiating, here are some things you can do:

1. Decide what sounds or silence you need and when you'll need these conditions.

2. Explain your needs in a way your partner, roommate, or housemate understands.

3. Listen to her needs.

4. Brainstorm mutually satisfying solutions. For example, you might study best at 3 A.M. with heavy metal music at full volume. That probably is too much to ask of a roommate, so you make some tapes or CDs for yourself and wear a headset.

5. Understand that circumstances can change. For example, you might need to extend your quiet time during exams, or she might need extra quiet from you right before her term paper is due.

6. Check in with her from time to time. Ask if you're holding up your part of the bargain, and tell her if she is or isn't holding up hers.

3.7 • If You're Having Difficulty Concentrating

It happens to all of us. The clock is ticking too loudly. The pretzels are calling to you. You've sharpened every pencil you own (plus others you've borrowed). You've cleaned the toilet and brushed the dog. You've done just about everything but your academic work.

You could decide to ignore the fact that your concentration is shaky or nonexistent, and plow on. It might return, and that would be great. If it doesn't return, try to analyze what's bothering you.

Some reasons for difficulty concentrating:

- You don't want to do the assignment, or you don't understand the assignment.

- You need exercise; maybe you've been sitting too long.

- You're homesick.

- You're worried that you can't do the kind of work you'd like to do, or you're afraid your best work won't be appreciated.

- You don't know where to start, or you have lots of ideas but you don't know how to organize them.

- You have too much to do and not enough time.

- Your environment or relationships are distracting you (your living situation is too noisy, you've just had a fight).

- You're broke.

- You have stopped believing in yourself, or you're starting to believe negative messages about yourself that you've heard from a few other people.

- You've just broken up with your significant other.

- You want your paper to be perfect.

All of these issues are addressed in this book. Look for them in the chapters to come.

 **HOT TIP!** *If you decide to take a break, don't feel guilty, or you'll lose whatever advantage that break could provide.*

3.8 • Don't Get Frustrated, Get Services

Schools offer incredible resources because they want you to finish your courses and do well. Take advantage of what you've already paid for through your tuition and fees. In particular, we recommend the tutoring center—*alias* the learning center, academic skills center, writing center, math center, and language place.

What happens during tutoring:

- You talk with tutors to explore how you learn best, how you can best tackle an assignment at hand, and how you can best manage your time.
- You get feedback from trained and supervised people who sincerely care about your progress.
- In the privacy of the tutoring session, you can ask questions that you might feel reluctant to ask in class.
- You identify your strengths and challenges, and find ways to work on both.
- You receive the support of someone who's "been there."

When to go for tutoring help in writing:

- You're stuck.
- You keep writing more and more and don't know when to stop.
- You're not sure your latest draft is better than your first.
- You don't know how to incorporate your mountains of notes into your paper.
- You can't find a topic for a paper.
- You don't know how to work with your professor's feedback.
- You're not sure which sources to use.
- You have a research paper that scares you.

When to go for reading tutoring:

- You're falling further and further behind.
- You read, but you're not absorbing. Or you absorb the material quickly, but forget it later.
- The reading is extremely different in relation to what you've done before.
- You want more strategies for effective reading.

When to go for math tutoring:

- You're missing some assignments.
- You have no (or little) idea how to do the homework.
- You haven't taken this math before and you're not on top of it.
- You want some new ways of tackling problems.

Questions to ask about tutoring services

1. What happens in a tutoring session?
2. Who will tutor you? If you want, can you get the same tutor each time?
3. How long are the sessions?
4. How many appointments are you allowed each semester and each week?
5. Is tutoring handled on a drop in or by appointment only basis?
6. What other services does the center offer?

HOT TIP!

It's best to go for tutoring long before your deadline approaches. We recommend checking out the tutoring center early in the semester just to get comfortable with the idea of using it. We have observed many times that the students who come to be tutored actually do quite well in school. In fact, the tutees (as we call them) often make terrific tutors! Many people say that tutoring is one of their most positive college experiences because their work gets so much attention. And, if you're the type who doesn't like the spotlight, remember that the focus is really on the process of learning and not particularly on your life and personal problems.

3.9 • Feed Your Head: Utilize the Library

The heart of any college is its library. Here you will find the resources you need to do research projects, access stimulating materials, and use critical equipment. Most libraries provide workshops, tours, and individual assistance to help you become comfortable and proficient. P.R.E.S.S. yourself to check out your college library's many resources:

People: Friendly, helpful staff. Reference librarians in particular can help you figure out how to do your research and find almost any piece of information.

Research sources: Books, professional journals, and newspaper and popular publications (both old and current) that will assist you in your research projects. Most libraries also have pamphlets that explain how to access what's available as well as tips for doing research. Also, many professors place materials at the reserve desk.

You will also find computer linkups that help you search for and download articles and on-line connections that let you identity resources available at other institutions where you have borrowing privileges. The Internet has powerful "search engines" that allow you to look for information faster and more precisely. (Be sure to learn your library's search engine system.)

Equipment: Computers, printers, and audio-visual technology, such as video and film equipment, overhead projectors, tape recorders, and copy machines for those materials you can't borrow. Look for special high- and low-tech adaptive equipment, which makes life a lot easier if you have a disability.

Special events: Lectures, films, and informative displays about cultural events, topical issues, and faculty work.

Special spaces: A relatively quiet, peaceful place to read or study. Libraries often have rooms that can be reserved for study groups.

Learn how to evaluate your research sources:
Just because something is in print or on the Internet doesn't automatically make it effective, accurate, or credible for your purposes.

Questions to help you decide on sources:

- Where was the material found? Where you access material depends largely on the nature of your topic. If your paper is on a controversial social issue, you will probably look at professional and popular journals and newspapers, but most likely not at encyclopedias (which tend to be overused by students as resources!). You might also interview people who have been closely involved in the issue.

- When was this material published? If you're working on a historical piece, a distant publishing date (say, 1932 or 1876) may be totally appropriate. If you're talking about computer technology, even material from last year may be outdated for your purposes.

- What do you know about the author? The material you use should be written by a credible source for the topic of your research. For a paper on manufacturing techniques, quoting from a machinist with a sixth-grade education might be more convincing than quoting from a sociologist.

- Is there a balance of points of view? Sometimes it's very helpful to use a variety of viewpoints. In a paper on capital punishment, you might want to include works by judges, victims' families, social workers, probation officers, children of criminals, or criminologists.
- Is there a range of sources? Unless your teacher tells you otherwise, it's probably best not to gather all your material from the same source, such as the same type of journal.

How to dig up sources:

- Begin to read in the field.
- Talk to others: your teachers, other students.
- Look at the bibliographies of articles and books that seem related to your project.

3.10 • How Sweet It Is: Entering College with Life Experience

Entering college as an adult learner has its advantages, even if you can't notice them right away.

Celebrate achievements that have brought you here:

- Realize that you have many strengths. Appreciate and use your life experiences: raising a family, being employed, keeping up a home or apartment, and/or being involved in your community.

- Remember your educational and career goals. These have propelled you into college and will keep you grounded.

- To help you persist, use your years of being with and observing people, of working through hard times. Know that persistence is critical to college success.

- Take pride in the fact that you are a life survivor and a risk taker: You're here in college now; many others have not made that choice.

- Take comfort in the fact that these years of living have introduced you to lots of ideas, helped you develop your vocabulary, and familiarized you with certain national and world events. This rich background will work for you in college.

Tips:

- Resist obsessing about being one of the oldest students.

- Try to stop seeing the other students as "kids." Get to know all your classmates as individual people.

- Find an ally, another student of any age with whom you can talk.

- Develop a realistic picture of how you're doing. Find ways to get the feedback you need from professors. Ask for occasional out-of-class conferences and specific comments on your papers and projects. Make full use of the official advising system, as well as whatever informal advising relationships you develop.

- Don't assume because you did poorly in a subject 10 or 30 years ago, you will repeat that experience. You're a different person now. Besides, teaching methods have greatly changed.

- Help your friends and family understand your experience. Develop a support network outside of school (as well as inside, of course).

- Find a place for yourself in the community of students. For example, returning students often make wonderful tutors.

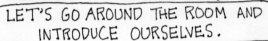

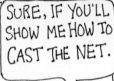

3.11 • If You Are an International Student

As an international student you may find college even more challenging—and possibly more rewarding—than your native-speaking peers. While all the information in this book will be useful to you, here are specific tips:

Communicate with your professors:

- Introduce yourself during the first week and explain that you are a non-native speaker.
- Find out what resources may be available, such as tutoring, videotaped material, and additional handouts.
- Ask professors if they are willing to give you copies of their notes or other aids to help you understand their classes.
- Ask your professors for study tips.
- Attend professors' office hours or make an appointment when you don't understand the class material or professors' feedback.
- Ask professors if you can audiotape their classes.

Communicate with your advisors and resource staff:

- Stay in contact with the foreign student advisor. Check before adding or dropping courses or applying for a work permit.
- Join a club for international students.
- Meet regularly with your academic advisor to plan a course schedule that will really work for you; keep discussing how you're doing. Remember that it might take you extra time to complete assignments.
- Don't forget that most schools provide health services if you're ill, and personal and career counseling when you need support.
- Utilize the tutoring center.

Communicate with other students:

- Be the first to say "hello," get to know other students, and help them get to know you. Each encounter can be a wonderful learning experience for both you and other students.
- Get a study buddy for each of your classes. Study together for exams, work on projects, and exchange class notes.
- Offer to make your favorite dish or talk about your culture. Many students enjoy learning about other countries.
- Volunteer to teach a friend how to speak some phrases from your first language and, in turn, get help in speaking, reading, or writing English.

How to work with the tutoring center:

- Join a conversation group in which you meet at least once a week to speak English with other non-native speaking students and a conversation leader. If there is no conversation group, ask if the center would consider organizing one.

- Understand the policy of the center regarding editing a students' work. Most, if not all, have a policy of not correcting your work for you. Instead, they tend to show you examples and provide helpful guidelines. Since practice is so important, try to attend individual tutoring sessions (or small group writing tutoring) at least twice a week, if possible.

- Realize that you may make the same mistake many times. This, of course, means it may take you more time to do assignments. The tutoring center can also help you work on your time management skills.

Other tips:

- Know what your bigger and smaller goals are. Remember, getting good grades and having papers with few mistakes are big goals, but there will probably be many others you will want to have along the way. As you reach your small goals, acknowledge them.

- Understand that you may be able to write better than you speak, or speak better than you write. Try to figure out what your strengths are and what you need to work on.

- Realize that when you're stressed or tired, you may make mistakes.

- Speak as much English at home as possible. Read English books and view English language TV.

- Know that an academic English paper may have different requirements than an academic paper in another language. Read samples of academic English papers that address the assignments you've been given.

Students who have been in the United States for a long time and who speak English quite fluently may still run into difficulties when reading complex material, writing essays, and doing research. Unfortunately, many times professors don't realize that these students may also be struggling. Don't be embarrassed to approach your professors and let them know you're having difficulties. And don't forget to seek out tutors to help you develop your skills.

3.12 • Close Encounters of the Extracurricular Kind

When you walk across the stage to get your college diploma, you will be a very different person from the one who first stepped onto campus. The people you meet and the activities in which you participate will contribute significantly to your development.

Extracurricular activities that take limited time:

- Sporting events
- Concerts, plays, gallery openings
- Movies
- Lectures by interesting and/or controversial speakers
- Dances, socials
- Open houses of the president, deans, departments
- Walking tours
- Evening or weekend outings with friends
- Religious services of many denominations

Extracurricular activities that involve more time and commitment:

- Clubs and associations
- Student government
- Sports
- A band or singing group
- Acting
- Campus newspaper or magazine
- On- or off-campus community service

Meeting new people:

- Challenge yourself to get to know people of different ages, ethnicities, social backgrounds, hometowns, and nationalities. (While it may be comfortable to hang out with people who are similar to you, it's probably not as interesting or thought provoking.)
- Become a conversation partner with an international student.
- Spend time with people who are older or younger than you.
- Sit with new people in the cafeteria or student union and invite new people to join your circle of friends.
- Strike up conversations with people in your classes who have very different points of view from yours (even if you disagree).

In your first year, you'll probably have little or no room for electives. Consider participating in extracurricular activities. They can give you some choice and variety and provide safe places to try out your strengths in another context as well as to develop your weaker areas. These activities can also help you learn about different cultures and styles, which is not only exciting but will also serve you well in the job market and in future social situations. Just remember to schedule those extracurricular activities on your calendar! And, of course, don't get so dazzled by all the possible activities that you lose sight of your coursework.

3.13 • A Beginner's Guide to Visualization

Visualization is a technique that lets you imagine and project yourself into any situation you would like to experience. Visualizing can often make a real difference in performance, as many Olympic and other world-class athletes can attest. There are many forms of visualization. We offer a very simple description and some tips.

A visualization scenario:

Problem: You have a big exam coming up. You're worried that you might freeze and that the results of the exam will not reflect your knowledge and all your hard work.

Solution: In addition to studying, you decide to visualize (mentally see yourself) taking the exam.

1. Sit in a comfortable position in a quiet place, close your eyes, and breathe slowly and deeply.

2. Consciously go through your body with your mind's eye and relax any areas of tension.

3. See yourself in the room where you will be taking the test. Add as many sensory details as you can. Hear the scratching of pens on paper, smell the peculiar smells of the classroom. Make the scene as real as you can.

4. Mentally see yourself getting a copy of the test questions, reading them, understanding them, and feeling focused and confident.

5. See yourself feeling calm and recalling and applying the material you studied.

6. Imagine yourself writing easily, feeling in control, and having more than enough time to finish the test.

7. Form mental images of yourself finishing your exam and feeling satisfied with your performance.

Some tips about visualization

Always focus on how you act and feel, not on what you might want other people to do. Using the exam example, don't visualize your professor giving you an A: You have no control over that. Instead, visualize yourself reading the question carefully and remembering relevant material.

Be as specific and as detailed as you can. The more you can include smells, tastes, sounds, movements, and visual details, the more effective the visualization will be.

Always focus on a positive outcome. (But also be realistic. Trying to visualize finishing the exam in five minutes may not be useful!)

You might find this technique difficult or awkward at first, but, like any skill, it takes practice. Visualization can be so effective, it's worth taking the time to learn.

 **HOT TIP!** *Visualizing is an aid to action, not a substitute for it. You still have to study.*

• *Activity 3.1*

Keep a "strengths journal" for one week. Each day, identify and describe one of your strengths, the circumstances under which you use it, and what happens as a result of your application of this strength.

● *Activity 3.2*

Review the cartoon in "Close Encounters of the Extracurricular Kind". If you were the main character, what would you say in the final frame? Draw or describe your-self in the situation. Or rewrite this cartoon as if Skip were the one who is thinking of expanding his horizons.

4

Managing Your Precious Time

Time is an essential resource. Most of us wish we had more and wish we did better with the time we've got. Learning to manage your time is one of the most important skills of the successful student.

The purpose of this chapter is for you to:

- Establish semester, monthly, weekly, and daily schedules
- Strengthen your skills in setting and maintaining priorities
- Develop a repertoire of time-management strategies for dealing with daily hindrances, such as phone interruptions, excessive TV, unwelcome visitors, and losing things
- Recognize and begin to overcome procrastination

4.1 • Scheduling for the Semester

One thing college won't put you into is a rut. Every week—every day!—brings something new. The places you have to be and the things you have to do are constantly changing. That's why creating and maintaining a schedule is so important: Without it you might find yourself, as one of our friends likes to say, "up the creek in a chickenwire canoe."

Make the most of your scheduling:

- Use a semester calendar with enough space to write five to eight items for each day, including weekends.
- Plot out all your class times, work schedule, family commitments, meetings, and any other significant time commitments (clubs, sports, picking up kids).
- Decide how long your travel time will need to be and block out those times as well.
- Look at each of your syllabi. Note all dates for tests, quizzes, projects, papers, reading assignments, and field trips.
- Use your college catalog and mark critical dates such as add/drop deadline, withdrawal deadline, mid-terms week, finals week, book returns, course registration, holidays, financial aid filing dates, and dorm room selection.
- Record personal dates such as birthdays of friends and family, anniversaries, and visits (to you and by you).

Select the semester calendar(s) that's right for you. Consider buying two: an erasable, laminated, wall-size, semester-at-a-glance calendar (sold by most stationery and office supply stores) and a portable daybook that's colorful, humorous, or in some other way fun to use. Use your calendar to express your individuality.

If you like gadgets, look into buying an electronic organizer. Also, don't forget that many computers have built-in schedulers.

 **HOT TIP!**

One of our very best pieces of advice: As soon as you get your course syllabi, student handbooks, and other official documents, start putting together a schedule. Trust us: You'll be much less stressed and much more successful.

4.2 • Making a Daily, Weekly, and Monthly Plan

You've got a general schedule for the semester. Now make it more effective by refining it.

Reasons to convert your semester schedule into a daily, weekly, and monthly schedule:

- As the semester progresses, you'll get to know your teachers better and develop your own pace for reading each of your textbooks. Once this happens, you'll have a much better idea of how much time you'll need to do your assignments.

- Your instructors will become more precise about your assignments as the semester goes on. As you get this information, you can plug it into your weekly and daily schedules.

- To keep yourself focused and ready to react to spur-of-the-moment invitations, suggestions, opportunities, and requests (as in, "Want a cup of coffee now?"), you have to be totally aware of your schedule day by day.

How to convert your semester schedule into a daily, weekly, or monthly schedule:

- Review your semester schedule for each week and also for each day.

- Look for those spaces that you have available for studying.

- Consider this general rule of thumb: For every hour of class, plan on studying between 2-1/2 and 4 hours.

- Take note of assignments due for the coming weeks and decide how much time you'll need for each. Some assignments might take one day; others might need more time. Working backwards from your due dates, plug in the time you need for each assignment.

- Try for some balance. For example, if you can manage it, don't put all the difficult reading assignments together in the same day. At the very least, try to alternate the work that is more challenging for you with the work that comes more easily.

How to fine-tune your daily schedule:

- Prepare yourself for each day by reviewing your schedule. Some people prefer to review their schedules in the morning; other people review the evening before.

- Consider the time, energy, space, and emotional resources it will take for you to accomplish each task. In your daily schedule, make sure you've included all those hidden time-busters (clearing off your desk so you can do your math homework, finding the handout that's buried, purchasing a toner for your printer, or getting to the computer lab to type and print your work).

- Carry your schedule and calendar with you. If deadlines are altered during class time, add these changes to your calendar immediately.

- Take a few minutes each day to evaluate how well your schedule has worked. Also, consider how well you have managed your schedule. Use this information to plan for the next day.

	Monday	Tuesday	Wednesday	Thursday	Friday	Saturday	Sunday
6:00	Alarm	Alarm	Alarm	Alarm	Alarm		
7:00	Get ready	Rev sched Commute	Get ready	Rev sched Commute	Get ready Commute	Alarm Get ready	
8:00	Rev.sched Commute	Math	Rev sched Commute	Math	Campus job	Laundry	
9:00	English	Walk to:	English	Library		Tel. calls Commute	
10:00	Coffee	Tutoring	Coffee			Off-campus	Clean
11:00	Comp. Sci.	Lunch	Comp. Sci.	Lunch		job	house Tennis &
12:00	Comp. Lab	J's gift	Comp. Lab		Lunch		brunch w/ John
1:00		Psych		Psych	Campus job	Lunch & read Eng	Begin
2:00	Lunch	Commute	Lunch	Hang out		Job	Psych reading
3:00	Appt. w/ Prof. H.	Relax!!!	Library: Math	See advisor			Work on
4:00	Commute Phone brk	English homework		Commute Start Eng	Tennis w/ John		Eng. paper
5:00	Study Math		Commute Cook &	paper	food shopping		Break
6:00	Cook & eat dinner	Dinner: take-out	eat dinner	Dinner: leftovers	Eng paper	Finish psych	Finish paper
7:00	Psych	Read Psych	Finish	Off-Campus	Dinner & movie out	Assignmnt Get ready	Prep.Mon Relax!!!
8:00	assignmnt	Comp. Appl.	Math	job		Jessie's birthday	
9:00	Math homework	Prepare for Wed.	Finish			party	
10:00	Prepare for Tues.	Relax!!	Psych Prep.Thur.	Prepare for Fri.			

4.3 • What's the Big Deal about Prioritizing?

You've got a thousand claims on your time. And your teachers keep demanding more. (We think it's our job!) Maybe you can't beat the system, but you can have a system for tackling your tasks. One significant method is prioritizing, that is, ordering what you have to do according to its importance.

Some ways to figure out your priorities:

- Look at your own balancing act.

- Check out all assignment due dates. Make sure that you're up-to-date with work due in your major.

- Look at your schedule and figure out what's important and what's immediate. They may not be the same. Keep reevaluating when things need to happen so that everything (or almost everything) gets done successfully.

- Ask yourself what would happen if you let go of one or more of the things on your list. (Weigh these consequences against the pressures of continuing it.)

- Talk over your priorities with friends, advisors, teachers, special others.

- Visualize what's most important to you.

- Take a moment to write about what's most important to you. Read what you've written.

- Pay attention to how you spend your time (and where you put your energy). Don't ask yourself what *should* I do, but what *do* I do. If you don't like what you see, then change it. For example, your goal might be to get the best grade you can in Spanish, but you never seem to have time to study. However, you spend two hours a day schmoozing over coffee with a friend. Is doing well in Spanish really your goal? If so, reduce your socializing and study your Spanish in the time you've saved.

How to make a daily priority schedule

Choose only three or four goals to accomplish, not 35. Choose priorities that are necessary but will be hard to accomplish unless you make a special effort. Don't focus on those goals that you know you'll do, no matter what. For example, if you know you will definitely go to class, select another goal.

Be as specific as you can. "Finish Soc" may not be as clear as "Read pages 10–17, then answer questions 1 and 2 on p. 17."

Select priorities that are in your control. "Get at least a B on English paper" is not totally up to you. But, "Make sure to include a complete bibliography, use spellchecker, and see a tutor to get feedback" are steps you can take to help you do your best work.

Ask yourself what needs to happen so you can achieve each priority. If writing a paper means being able to work at your desk, but it's piled high with papers and books, then you'll need to straighten up.

Be flexible. Things do come up, and there is usually more than one way to accomplish something.

4.4 • Deciding How Much To Study

How much you should study depends on both the task (or assignment) and you.

Here are some questions to help you figure out how much to study:

Purpose

- How clear are you about the assignment's purpose and requirements? (The clearer you are, the easier it will be.)

Reading Assignments

- How much reading are you expected to do?

- How thoroughly do you need to do it? Getting an overview might be easier than having to learn all the information.

- What type of reading do you have to do? Readings that contain lots of examples and stories tend to be easier than more abstract or theoretical material. Readings in your major or an elective might be more appealing to you and, therefore, seem less time consuming.

- What format is the reading in? Dense text with tiny margins might be more difficult to read than pages with lots of space, subheadings, and shorter paragraphs.

Writing Assignments

- How much experience do you have with the type of writing assigned? If the assignment is similar to one you've done before, it may demand less time.

- How familiar are you with the topic of your assignment? How much background information do you already have? Your knowledge of a topic can really help you complete the assignment.

- How formal or informal is this assignment? The less formal an assignment—a journal entry, notes, rough draft—generally, the easier it is.

- How complete does the assignment have to be? If the assignment has to be carried into several drafts, it will take more time. (For most assignments, you'll work through more than one draft.)

- How well researched does this assignment have to be? Generally, the more research, the more time you'll need.

- How long does the work have to be? Sometimes the shorter something needs to be, the less time it takes (but not always).

- How many different parts does the assignment have, and how complicated is each part? The more complex the parts are, the more time you may need. The number of parts is not always the best indicator of the amount of time you'll need.

- How personal does the writing have to be? For some students, writing about themselves is very difficult and, therefore, requires a lot of time. For others, personal writing comes more naturally.

4.5 • How To Have a Gourmet Study Session

Managing your time extends to how you run your own private study sessions. Think of them as gourmet meals, with enticing appetizers, hearty main courses, and tasty desserts.

Appetizers:

Study appetizers must get you to the table (or desk) where you need to study. Any short, nonharmful exercise or activity will do; it doesn't have to be very (or at all) related to the homework or study tasks you'll be doing during your study session. The critical thing about appetizers is that they help you transition into study mode without distracting you.

Examples of appetizers:

- Spending a few minutes reading your favorite magazine
- Writing notes to yourself about the assignment you'll be tackling
- Finding your papers or calendar
- Sitting in the chair in which you'll study
- Getting yourself something to drink or a snack

Main courses:

The main course is the set of academic activities you do during your actual study session.

- In any one time period, don't overwhelm yourself.
- Review your assignments and decide which you'll tackle and in what order. You might also want to give yourself a time limit for each. Some people like to check off the assignments or tasks as they are accomplished.
- For each assignment or task, make a plan. Try writing it down so you can see it.
- Find a way to monitor yourself (alarm watch, timer) so that you don't spend so much time on one task that you have no time for the rest.
- Stretch or do some physical activity every hour or so.

Dessert:

The study session dessert is the flavorful topping to a good meal. The idea is to choose or create a dessert that complements the meal without overwhelming it. So, choose a reward that is brief and helps you savor (or remember) what you've just accomplished.

Study rewards:

- Find those things you've done especially well.
- Tell someone else what you've accomplished.
- Remember how you organized the study session and how you managed your time throughout it; consider future adjustments you might make.
- Do something physical.
- Listen to music.

Even a plain meal can be made more tasty. When you have to study something uninteresting, create a nice environment with candles, flowers, your favorite objects or music. Organize your study space so it works for you.

4.6 • How To Get Friends and Family To Support Your Schedule

College makes demands on you, but also on the people closest to you. Suddenly everyone, including you, has to adjust to your schedule. Help the people in your life support what you have to do and when you have to do it by communicating clearly.

Don't expect people to support you if they don't know what's going on:

- Make sure your family and friends know your schedule. Give them copies and display it someplace—on a mirror or the refrigerator, near a phone—where people can see it.

- Explain when you need to leave for class and when you'll be back, as well as the consequences of having back-to-back classes (you might be tired), long classes (ditto), no breaks (ditto), or no time for lunch (ditto).

- Make sure to talk about how projects that are due just before anniversaries, birthdays, and other special occasions might affect the way you choose to celebrate (or delay celebrating).

- If you have Friday afternoon or Saturday classes, point out how these may affect your weekends.

- Make sure to discuss your schedule each time it changes (usually every quarter or semester).

- Know your limits. Try not to take on more social or family obligations than you can manage.

Notice the people who don't support your schedule and those who do

Try spending more time with those who are respectful of your schedule and less time with those who aren't. Understand that some people might:

Drop in late or when you're studying even when you've told them you're unavailable

Put pressure on you to go out when you can't

Monopolize your time or schedule things for you without your approval

Try to distract you by making loud noises, turning on the TV, talking to you, or otherwise interrupting your concentration

Act disappointed by changes in your schedule

Move your papers, books, or notes without your permission

4.7 • Getting Up and Out on Time

Getting where you need to be on time doesn't have to be a struggle or a frantic, aerobic exercise.

Some Reasons You Might Be Chronically Late, and Some Strategies to Try:

Can't wake up	• Set up two alarm clocks, one across the room. • Purchase a light that keeps getting brighter. • Ask a friend to give you a wake-up call. • Go to sleep earlier. • Do something fun to start the day. • Stay on a routine sleep schedule to fall asleep faster.
You and/or your children can't find something to wear	• Hunt for clothing the night before or consider organizing clothes for the entire week. • If desperate, have children sleep in sweatsuits so they'll be dressed in the morning. • Get up earlier to find clothes. • Assess your (or your children's) wardrobe during a more relaxed time and take action. (Give clothes away, swap, buy new things.)
Missing items	• Get yourself organized the night before. • At the beginning of the semester, make a list of items you'll need to bring for each weekday. • Keep list handy and refer to it daily. Post list by the door. • Use a separate book bag for each day or days with the same schedule. (For example, if your Mondays and Wednesdays require the same materials, designate a Monday/Wednesday book bag.)
Misplaced keys, glasses, etc.	• See "How to Stop Losing Things."
Get distracted by roommates or family	• Let everyone know the plan ahead of time, verbally or with signs.
Lose track of the time	• Be realistic about the amount of time you need. Don't start a big task if you only have few minutes. • Set a really loud timer so that it goes off every 10 minutes or goes off when you have 10 minutes left before you must head out the door.
Feel groggy	• Do some physical activity.
Besieged by unwanted calls	• Let answering machine screen calls.
Still doing homework	• Make a choice: Finish your work or leave on time.
	• If this is a pattern, discuss it with a friend, tutor, advisor, teacher.

HOT TIP! *Lateness suggests a lack of caring about class or about making friends or faculty wait. If you do care, but you're just disorganized, then try to fix the problem.*

4.8 • Answering Machine Follies and Other Ways To Defeat Interruptions

Just because someone calls or knocks on your door doesn't mean you have to interrupt what you're doing. Feel free to make creative use of the telephone and other devices to screen, delay, limit, ward off, or otherwise manage your interactions, especially during crunch times.

Methods for dealing with interruptions:

- Identify who your interrupters are and have a discussion with them before the crunch hits.

Use your answering machine:

- Let your answering machine screen calls even when you're home. Ask yourself whom you really need or want to answer. If you've already decided that nothing is worth your time at this moment, then lower the volume so you won't be tempted to pick up the phone.

Create an answering machine message to entertain but gently discourage others, such as:

- "I've gone into study mode and will be returning periodically. Leave messages only if desperate."
- "The library beckons me. I've gone into the stacks for the next three weeks."
- "I'm eating, sleeping, and dreaming my research paper on creativity. If you have any information about it, let me know in your voice message."

Leave messages on voice mail/e-mail instead of having conversations:

- Call when someone is likely to be out. Don't suggest a return phone call unless you really want to talk.

Manage drop-in visitors:

- Delegate a task to your visitors, such as stapling, sorting, helping you find a lost item, or something particularly gross like cleaning the toilet. They'll get the idea that you're busy, and you'll also get some extra help.
- Contain conversations by announcing at the beginning how much time you can spend and periodically reminding your visitors of this timeframe during the conversation. At the end of the your time limit, stand up and announce that you've got to get back to your work.
- Defer the visit to another time, when you know you either have more flexibility or can keep the conversation short (for example, in between your classes, when you have just 20 minutes).
- Redirect visitors to someone else who has more time or who can respond more fully.

Use signs:

Make a clock face with a movable arrow to indicate when you'll be available. Other examples include:

Student at Work; Steal Silently Away

Toll: $5.00 to Enter.

Work Construction in Progress. Enter at Your Own Risk.

Rabid Raccoon Trapped in Room.

4.9 • Taming TV

In a time of stress or confusion, it's easy to turn to TV. You don't have to take notes; it won't give you a quiz or even a homework assignment. But TV can also be a big time sinkhole. If you're watching more TV than your schedule can afford, consider the following.

When TV watching might need taming:

- You find yourself spending more and more time in front of the TV and less time socializing. In fact, you prefer TV to personal contact.
- Watching TV, you feel mesmerized and almost immobile, all the time knowing you have other things to do.
- No matter how much TV you watch, no program ever feels very satisfying and yet you continue to watch more.
- You tell yourself you can shut the TV off at any time, but you don't.
- You're falling farther and farther behind in school and not getting the grades you want.
- TV feels more important than the world around you.
- You notice that in times of stress you turn on the TV and then it just stays on.

Sometimes TV watching is really a symptom of:

- Being lost in college
- Anxiety about not doing as well as you'd like
- Feeling overwhelmed by the amount or type of work you have
- Homesickness or longing for the life you had before college
- Questioning your goals or career path

Taming strategies:

- Hide the remote control.
- Make a pact with yourself about the amount of TV you'll watch.
- First do your work, then use the TV as a reward.
- Find other ways to relax or vary your routine when you get the urge to turn on the TV.
- Try studying in places that don't have TVs.
- Hide your TV; disconnect it; give it away.
- Consider going to the counseling center.

While there has been a lot of debate about the effect of TV on violent behavior, TV can have another, less publicized influence. Many TV programs describe a world where relationships are simple and all problems get solved before the last commercial. If you are beginning to compare your friends, love, school, and work relationships to the ones you see on TV, remember: Those people are actors! They have scripts! Don't buy the fantasy.

4.10 • How To Stop Losing Things

Okay, so you don't lose things. Maybe you creatively misplace them. Or maybe you're like most people: The more stress you're under, the more things you can't find.

Some tips:

- Figure out what you tend to misplace the most. Keys, glasses, class notes, address books, calendars, bills, and other notices are often on the "Most Wanted" list.

- Create a system for storing and retrieving each item. This system could include finding a consistent place and time to put things. For example, place keys on the same hook as soon as you walk in the door.

- Find (or make) special spots for keeping those things most-likely-to-turn-up-missing. For traveling, your address book could always go in a particular compartment in your backpack or purse.

- Stick to your system. Make it a habit. Tell someone about it. The more you repeat your system, the more it becomes a conscious part of your routine, and the less chance you have of misplacing any item.

- Try making a list of what you need to bring to school for each day. (You may need a different list for different days.) That way you won't have to guess or take the time to remember. Make sure to check this list before you head out the door. If you know you'll be having a particularly difficult day, try packing up the night before. If you have children living with you, help them use this system or one like it.

- Remember, being in a hurry or feeling stressed tends to divert your attention. Consequently, during these times you'll be more likely to misplace things. Recognize that especially during crunch times your mind will be on your projects, tests, quizzes, and papers; so give yourself a little extra time to pack or prepare for the day.

- Once you've misplaced an item, try to retrace your steps, at least mentally. Even though it's hard, refrain from panicking—that will only make things worse.

4.11 • Overcoming Procrastination I: The Truth behind the Excuse

Your paper was assigned weeks ago. You need to get a really good grade! You don't know much about the topic, aren't sure how to get started, and, frankly, you're terrified of the library research this work requires. This paper is just too important to mess up. The more time that goes by, the more fearful you get, and the more it seems that you'll never get started. You now have only two days before this 15-page paper is due. Your pulse is racing, and you kick yourself for procrastinating—again—as you finally begin.

Does this sound even a little bit familiar? If so, welcome to Procrastinators Anonymous, an organization with a secret membership of millions.

Procrastination excuses:

Excuse 1: I don't know how to start, so I'll wait until I get all the information.
   Instead: Take the time with every assignment to find out if it involves several steps. Break them down, create a timeline, and do one step at a time.

Excuse 2: I've got to get a good grade on this (paper, project, whatever). It's too important to mess up. I can't start until I've thought of the best approach.
   Instead: Thinking about the best approach may only get you so far, especially if weeks (or days) have gone by and nothing's happening. Try something—anything. If that doesn't work, try something else.

Excuse 3: I don't know how to deal with libraries (select whatever fits here). I'm waiting until this feeling passes, or at least until I'm so busy I don't notice it.
   Instead: The feeling might not pass. Find a buddy and go to the library together. Talk to someone (a friend, a counselor, your advisor). Don't keep the feeling bottled up. The longer it sits, the bigger it gets.

Excuse 4: I've got to do it right. It's got to be perfect.
   Instead: Sorry, but perfection doesn't exist. Doing an assignment well is certainly possible, but waiting won't make that happen. If the paper or project is important (or your grade depends on it), then most likely it will need several revisions. That takes time and hard work, not just wishing.

Some students say they work well under pressure. They like the kind of excitement or state of mind they're in when they block everything else out and stay up all night to write a paper or cram for an exam. Some people do need that kind of intensity and are willing to pay the price, whatever it might be.

However, you might want to consider the latest research into memory. Researchers have found that cramming does not create the strong physical connections in the brain that allow you to retain knowledge. That's why cramming usually means that whatever you learn is almost immediately lost. Studying over a period of time establishes strong memory connections, and so you more effectively retain what you've learned.

4.12 • Overcoming Procrastination II: Other Ways To Beat It

1. Make a contract with yourself. Give yourself a reward for working either a certain period of time or for doing a certain assignment or part of an assignment. Start small, then build up.

2. Set a routine. Start attacking the big assignment by building it into your daily schedule.

3. Especially when you're working on big projects, make reminder signs for yourself and place them on your mirrors, doors, refrigerator, closets, windows. Use funny Post-its®.

4. Study (or work on your project) with a friend who is able to get things done. Make a study time and place that works for both of you. Agree on how much (or how little) you'll talk. Sometimes just silent companionship is enough to get you started.

5. Try studying with a friend on the telephone. At a pre-arranged time, call your friend. Once you reach him, put the receiver on a table and start working. Set a time to check in with each other. However, don't try this if you share a phone with other people or if it's a long distance call (unless you have a trust fund).

6. If you're procrastinating about talking to a teacher or another student because you're shy, afraid, or intimidated, rehearse. Here are four ways: rehearse by yourself (you could also try this in front of a mirror); rehearse with a friend (who can also help you construct some lines); rehearse by writing out the conversation. Some find it helpful to use a play format: Put the names of the players in the margins, followed by their lines; rehearse by taping the conversation.

7. Ease into it. Make a deal with yourself that you'll spend five minutes on the task or assignment. Just five measly little minutes! You might get interested and continue beyond this limit.

Procrastination Games

The Quick Version: Give yourself a point for each minute (or five minutes) that you're working. Fifteen point game.

Version Two: Give yourself one point for doing something easy, three points for doing something a little more difficult and ten points for the most difficult part of the project or task. Don't stop until you've reached 20 points.

Version Three: Keep a running game going over a few sessions or days. Work out a 100-point system. Give yourself a big reward at the end.

4.13 • How To Find Time You Didn't Think You Had

Using even small chunks of time to do bits of your coursework can have a big payoff. The key is being prepared. Always have some relevant material with you, should that stray five minutes suddenly appear. The time is there if you just look for it. During the course of a day or a week it can add up. Remember, the time you save might be time you can spend having fun.

You can find hidden time while you're:

- Sitting in a waiting room or picking someone up
- Riding public transportation
- Stuck in traffic (If you're driving, you can listen to relevant tapes.)
- Doing laundry
- On hold
- Backing-up computer files
- Waiting through a pro football or basketball commercial break
- Having a cup of coffee
- Between classes

Things you can do with 10 to 15 minutes:

Re-read the instructions for your next paper or other assignment.

Read the Table of Contents and Index of a required text.

Read one section of an article.

List the key points you've just read.

List the day's errands.

List some questions to ask in class.

Review the class schedule.

Straighten up your study space.

4.14 • Four Ways (Plus One) To Make Better Use of Your Time

There probably isn't a person alive who couldn't manage her time more effectively. The trick is to experiment. If something isn't working, keep making adjustments. Here are four ways to make better use of your time.

1. Avoid unnecessary trips to your dorm room or car.
It's easy to forget that the time it takes you to travel back and forth from your dorm room or car is real time: It adds up. Instead of returning to your room two or three times a day between classes to study, bring some work with you and find a place close to your classroom. If the weather is changeable, bring a sweater or an umbrella and save yourself a trip.

2. Plan for contingencies.
Especially if you're a commuter student, keep extra copies of your syllabi and calendar. Keep a list of telephone numbers you're likely to need. Bring back-up disks with you and know where computers and printers are located.

3. Decide whether or not you can do two things at once.
Realize that tasks need different kinds of attention. For example, you might have no trouble chopping vegetables while talking on the phone, but find it impossible to talk on the phone and work in your sketchbook at the same time. Be realistic about assessing what you actually can do.

4. Color code.
Buy paper, notebooks, and file folders separately color-coded for each class. Bright colors might help keep you awake, too.

Plus one

If you're becoming tired or bored during a study session, try alternating tasks. For example, if you've been reading something theoretical, switch to doing something more physical (copying over your notes), artistic (doing a sketch for your art class), or hands-on (working on the computer). Try different time blocks. If an hour is too long, try working in 30-minute spurts. If you've been sitting, try standing, stretching, or taking a brief walk. Switch chairs, study carrels, or rooms.

● Activity 4.1

Using as large a sheet of paper as you need, develop a semester calendar for yourself. Mark all your classes, project dates, test dates, internship or work hours, and important school dates. Make sure to include all your study times, commuting times, plans for weekend trips, and anything else that applies. After you have created this calendar, write one to two paragraphs about the challenges your schedule presents. Then write one to two paragraphs on what action steps you can take to address these challenges.

● *Activity 4.2*

Look at the cartoon in "What's the Big Deal About Prioritizing?" If there were a fifth frame, what would it contain? Now, either draw the fifth frame or, if you prefer, simply write the dialogue that you imagine would take place.

5

Power Reading and Notetaking

You can't get through college without effective reading and notetaking skills. Notetaking can really enhance your reading ease and comprehension, and reading will open doors and worlds to you.

The purpose of this chapter is for you to:

- Learn how to begin a reading assignment
- Develop the power tools of finding your purpose, asking questions, identifying the main points, and summarizing
- Acquire effective notetaking methods, including marginal notes, personal reading journals, and mapping
- Increase your confidence and skill in creating and understanding charts

5.1 • Reading: It's a Job!

College reading can be much more challenging than career-related or high-school reading. In college you will probably have more material to read, and it will be denser, more abstract or theoretical. On top of that, most college professors won't remind you to keep up. There are many things you can do to develop college reading skills. The first step is to think of reading as a skilled job, one that has definite responsibilities, qualifications, and benefits.

Wanted: Individual Eager To Become Good Reader; On-the-job Training Available

General information

Good readers do not have to read fast, possess huge vocabularies (at least at the start of their first year in college), or come from exclusive private schools. Contrary to popular opinion, many people who have become good readers were not born that way. Successful readers know that reading better is a lifelong process; they learn how to use their college experience to read more effectively. Although careful reading is often a prerequisite to high grades, a good reader gets much more than a grade from the reading.

Responsibilities of a reader:

1. Develops many strategies for making sense of different kinds of material (magazine and newspaper articles, syllabi, class handouts, textbooks, novels, manuals, reference books) and different subjects (history, chemistry, English, computer applications)

2. Determines what's most important and doesn't try to memorize every detail

3. Uses a variety of approaches when reading; when one method doesn't work, moves to another

4. Actively learns new vocabulary

5. Is not afraid to disagree with the text; on the other hand, is willing to think carefully about it before ignoring it or minimizing its importance

Qualifications:

1. Curious, patient, and persistent

2. Willing to adjust reading habits as needed

3. Willing to keep checking how much he understands

4. Sense of humor always a plus (especially an ability to laugh at oneself)

Benefits:

An enormous asset to achieving college, career, and even interpersonal goals; can be one of life's greatest pleasures

Why you should care about what you read

You don't have to love the material you're reading, but if you are willing to follow the author's line of reasoning, approach, and examples, if you're willing to give the author a chance and try to relate the text to other material you've read or heard about, you'll probably remember more material longer. There has been lots of research on how quickly we forget (80% within 24 hours, if we don't reinforce the material!). Researchers find that when we start to think about the material and relate it to our experience (or others' experiences), our memory for the material is greatly enhanced.

5.2 • Identifying a Purpose for Your Reading

Finding a purpose (or purposes) for reading is like going on a car trip with a good map. It allows you to find the best roads, shortcuts, and landmarks, and helps you avoid taking wrong turns and getting frustrated.

Suppose you have an assignment such as "Read Chapter 6." Some possible purposes include:

- Get a general idea or overview of what it covers
- Prepare for a test or quiz on the material
- Answer the questions in the back of the chapter
- Be prepared to discuss your views of the material
- Raise questions in class about what you didn't understand

You'll probably read the material differently depending on your purpose.

PURPOSES	WHAT YOU CAN DO
Overview	• Preview, review table of contents, skim the material, get a feeling for the kind of topics covered
Prepare for a test or quiz	• Review class notes; analyze the questions asked in your quizzes and homework assignments; read and summarize any of your professor's comments on your work to date, identify material that seems likely to capture your professor's interest, turn that material into questions, and answer those questions
Answer questions in the back of the chapter	• Read questions first, preview, locate information that will answer the questions, make notes (see 5.7) or marginal comments (see 5.8) to help you fully comprehend the material
Raise questions in each class about the material you didn't understand	• Preview, find the main point of each section, ask yourself questions as you go along, use margins to identify confusing material

Hey, it's Mr. Question-Person !

Each week Mr. Question-Person roams the campus armed with only a notebook and camera, seeking answers to today's hard student questions. He strikes without warning, so watch out: maybe this week you'll find yourself in Mr. Question-Person!

This week's question: *If you have to re-read a chapter to prepare for a test, how would you do it?*

Jean-Paul E.
Major:
Philosophy

"Assuming their existence, I would read the summary and answer the questions at the back of the chapter."

Chen L.
Major:
Art

"I'd look at the material through the professor's eyes to see what might make a good question. I hope that's not too abstract."

Nathan J.
Major:
Computer
Science

"I would simply re-read the entire chapter, review my notes, talk with the professor, and create my own sample exam. Did I forget anything?"

Pearl Z.
Major:
French Lit.

"Don't bother me. I'm just getting to the good part!"

5.3 • How To Begin a Reading Assignment

Let's say you have to read a chapter in a textbook and answer two questions. You can take a deep breath, plow in, and just start to read. But, using this approach is like turning yourself into a couch potato, only with a book instead of a TV. There's a better way. We suggest a two-prong approach: getting a grip on the exact instructions for your assignment, and giving yourself an orientation or preview of the material.

The first step: Get a grip on the assignment

1. Reread the assignment instructions. Try to pinpoint exactly what your professor expects you to get from the reading. Whatever the assignment instructions, turn them into a purpose for reading.

2. If you are supposed to use the reading to answer questions or do problems, be absolutely sure you understand them. Sometimes this means reading the questions or problems several times. Once you understand the questions or problems, highlight key words or rewrite the questions or problems in your own words.

The second step: Give yourself an orientation

Take five to fifteen minutes to survey the chapter, article, or handout to get a feeling for the kinds of information the author has included and the order of this information. Here are the steps to follow:

1. Read the outline, objectives, summary, and conclusion.

2. Read the introduction, the subheadings, charts, or tables.

3. Read the first paragraph under each subheading.

4. Especially if this material feels intimidating, try holding the book or handout in your hands. Touching the pages can reduce fear.

5. Now you're ready to begin reading the assignment.

Before beginning your first reading assignment in a book, take the time to preview the book itself.

Check out the title (which can give you valuable information about the scope and slant of the book) and scan the Table of Contents.

Read the Preface so you can figure out the kinds of material the author will and will not cover in the text.

Thumb through the book and look for any special features of the text.

Some authors use bold, italic, or capitalization; some put boxes around, number, or bullet important points. In this text we've used a combination of all these techniques.

5.4 • Finding Main Points

Getting the main idea or main point is essential to comprehending any reading that is assigned to you. Each sentence, paragraph, page, section, and book has a main point. If you're reading complex material, you might want to read one section at a time, stop, and identify the main point of each section before moving on.

The technique of finding the main idea works especially well when you're reading heavily factual material, new terminology, philosophical or abstract text, a new subject, or a foreign language. It also can work well if you're feeling impatient, cranky, distracted, or if you can't sit still.

Here are some things you can do to find the main idea:

- Look at the title or subheadings.
- Make a list of the specific facts or other information included in the passage.
- Identify key words. (Write them, underline, circle, or highlight.)

Ask yourself questions:

- What's the most important point? How do I know?
- What is all the information in the passage about?
- What is the common theme or thread that ties all the information together?
- Is there a sentence that expresses the main point?

Using any (or all) of the above, write a sentence that contains the main idea of the passage.

What does a main idea sentence look like?

A main idea sentence very concisely summarizes all the key information in a passage. Here's how we could express the main idea of this section up to this point:

"Getting the main idea is essential to reading comprehension, and there are at least five ways to figure out the main idea."

Here are some ineffective ways to describe the main idea of this section:

- Reading comprehension (*extremely general*)
- Finding the main idea is important to reading comprehension. (*Covers only part of the material on this page.*)
- You have to work hard to find the main point. (*This is an opinion.*)

Suggestions for writing your own main idea:

- Use a sentence instead of a phrase.
- Be patient if you don't get it right away. This skill takes time to develop.
- Remember, if you have a strong reaction to the material, you might misinterpret what the author is trying to say. First, find out what the main point really is (not, for example, how it makes you feel) and save your personal reactions for later in the process.

Other ways to use main ideas

Visuals: To find the main idea of a cartoon, chart, or graph, ask yourself questions like: What pattern do I see? What is this visual primarily talking about?

Your own writing: Look over your writing and examine each paragraph for the main idea. If you find more than one main point in a paragraph, you might have included too much information. If you can't tell what the main point is, you may need to rethink what you're trying to say.

● HOT TIP! *The technique of identifying the main idea works very well in combination with summarizing, all forms of notetaking, and many test preparation methods.*

5.4 Finding Main Points   93

5.5 • Asking Questions

You'll beat the odds of falling asleep (plus you'll retain what you've read a lot longer) if you stay involved in the process of reading. One way to do this is to ask yourself questions *as* you're reading. These questions give you a focus and reduce the chances of daydreaming about something else or finding your mind on automatic pilot.

Questions that help you relate what you're reading to your experience and opinions:

- What do I already know about this topic?
- How is this subject related to my major?
- How is this subject related to my other courses?
- How is this subject related to other things I've read?
- How does this passage relate to the course, the last class, or the rest of the reading assignment?
- What do I think of this idea (concept, method, fact)?
- What sentence in this paragraph seems to stand out the most? Why?
- What do I like most about this passage? Why?
- What do I like least about this passage? Why?
- What is the author saying just below the surface?

Questions about the main point:

- What's the main point of this paragraph? Section? Chapter?
- What's least important to this passage? Why?
- What does all this add up to?

Questions about the author:

- What do I know about the author? (For example, is the author biased in one way or another?)
- Why did the author write this?
- If the author were right here, what would I want to ask him or her?

Questions about facts:

- What practices, theories, rules, methods are being discussed?
- Who are the significant people involved? What information is given about them?
- What are the steps or stages being discussed?
- Are all the steps given?
- Are all the steps equally important?

Questions that predict:

- What do I think the author will say next?
- What do I want to remember?
- Which information might show up on a quiz?

Questions that help you keep track of what you're reading:

- How do I know I understand the material?
- What is confusing?
- What new vocabulary am I learning?
- What new information have I just learned?

Adjust these questions and devise your own!

You might find yourself changing these questions or creating new ones as you read in different disciplines. Also, keep in mind that sometimes you might ask only one or two questions in a whole section, while at other times you'll ask yourself many.

5.6 • Summarizing

A summary is a condensed version of a text (book, article, handout, speech, video, etc.) usually in paragraph form. To write a summary, pare down the text to its most essential points.

How to write a summary:

- Survey the text by looking at the introduction, objectives and subheadings.
- Identify the main point of each section.
- Look at the amount of space the author devotes to different topics. Chances are, the more space allocated, the more important a topic is.
- From this list of main points, identify the three to five most important points in the whole piece.
- If you have trouble identifying the main points, reread any sections you need to.
- Write your summary. Sometimes it helps to read it out loud.
- Revise, as needed.
- Make your summary approximately one-quarter of the length of the original passage (but don't get too concerned about length unless your professor sets a limit).

Original Text

> The first major metropolis in Central America was the city of Teotihuacan, capital of an early kingdom that arose sometime around the third century b.c.e. and flourished for nearly a millennium until it collapsed under mysterious circumstances about 800 c.e. Located about 30 miles northeast of Mexico City, Teotihuacan covered an area of at least eight square miles and had as many as 150,000 inhabitants during its heyday. Along its main thoroughfare were temples and palaces, all dominated by a massive Pyramid of the Sun rising in four tiers to a height of over 200 feet. In the vicinity are the remains of a large market where goods from distant regions, as well as agricultural produce grown by farmers in the vicinity, were exchanged.
>
> Living within the fertile Valley of Mexico, an upland plateau surrounded by magnificent snow-capped mountains, the inhabitants of Teotihuacan probably obtained the bulk of their wealth from agriculture. At that time, the valley floor was filled with swampy lakes containing the water runoff from the surrounding mountains. The combination of fertile soil and adequate water combined to make the valley one of the richest farming areas in Central America.

Summary

> Thirty miles from Mexico City, Teotihuacan was the first major Central American metropolis, and a rich farming area from the 3rd century b.c.e. until 800 c.e. Comprised of more than 8 square miles and populated by 150,000 inhabitants, Teotihuacan included temples, palaces, and a large market for agricultural exchange when the city collapsed mysteriously.

(*Source:* William J. Duiker and Jackson J. Spielvogel, *World History Volume I: To 1800*, Minneapolis/St. Paul, MN: West Publishing Company, p. 463)

Other tips:

- Be aware that you are making choices of what to include as well as what to exclude.
- Do not include your opinion.
- Incorporate enough material so you have a miniature version of the original text. Don't provide a lot of smaller detail.

Summarizing will work well by itself and also in combination with mapping and other forms of notetaking, list making, freewriting, making marginal comments, and other methods. Summarizing chapters or your notes is an excellent exam preparation method.

HOT TIP! *Professors do tend to have different ideas about what summary writing is, so ask them if they have specific guidelines.*

5.7 • The Knack of Notetaking

Imagine this: It's the night before your big exam on five chapters. You have already read the text pretty thoroughly so you're feeling confident. But, as you start to review the material, it looks completely foreign. You think, "I've never even seen these pages! Did I read this in some other life?" Then, you start to panic.

You really can avoid this bang-your-head-against-the-wall moment by taking notes when you read. Making and reviewing your notes reinforces what you're learning, helps you remember it better, and assists you in sorting out what's important.

Examples of what to include in your notes:

- Main ideas or summaries of each section
- Important principles, rules, names, dates, and/or formulas
- New terms and their definitions
- Your reactions

You have many options for organizing your notes, such as:

- Paragraphs
- Maps
- Marginal comments
- Audiotaping
- Personal reading journal

When to take your notes:

- *Immediately* after you've finished reading a chapter or a section, in order to check how much you've understood and to reinforce that material in your mind
- *As* you read to help you stay focused and keep on track
- Some combination of these two

When to review your notes:

- *Right after you've taken them.* At this point you can make sure you've included all the information you want, checked for clarity and organization, and reinforced your memory.
- *Every two to five days.* The review should also include writing additional notes as you discover how the material from one section is related to material from another.

An example of notes from this page (we've chosen to use a paragraph)

Notes can include main ideas of each section, new terms, definitions, personal reactions, and summaries. Options for organizing notes include paragraphs, charts, maps, or marginal comments. Notes can be taken immediately after reading, while you're reading, or some combination of these approaches. Notes also need to be reviewed immediately after they're written and every two to five days after that.

5.8 • Using the Margins

Okay, so you've been told never to write in your books. You don't believe every-thing you hear, do you? Margins are excellent places to keep track of your thoughts as you read. Many books now feature enlarged margins just for this purpose.

What you might write in the margins:

- Questions to the author ("Why did you write that?" "How is paragraph 2 connected to paragraph 3?")
- Questions to yourself
- Vocabulary and definitions
- Main points of each paragraph or section
- Examples from your life that relate to the text
- Comments about the author's style, organization, graphics
- Phrases you like or that make you think
- Diagrams or sketches of the material
- Your disagreements and agreements with the author
- Your ideas for tackling an assignment
- Abbreviations such as *imp* for "important information" or *T* for "professor mentioned this could be on the test"

When to write marginal notes:

- *As* you go along. Marginal notes are especially helpful when you're reading long, technical paragraphs, sections, or chapters, and you're having trouble keeping all the information in your head (or the author is making it hard for you).
- *After* you've read a section. This technique works especially well for summarizing material or when you prepare to answer assignment questions.
- Both *as you go along* and then *after* each section.

Why marginal notes sometimes work better than regular notes:

- You don't have to interrupt the flow of your reading by trying to find writing paper.
- There's less chance of losing marginal notes (unless you lose the book).
- They're more convenient to do. You don't have to give page or paragraph numbers; you can circle or underline relevant points and write your own comments next to them.
- You don't have to say as much because there's less space.
- You're thinking about the material as you're reading, so writing marginal notes can help you comprehend more efficiently.
- Your notes are right next to the text they reference, so you can go back and forth easily.

You can also make marginal comments on your own writing to help you revise. Writing these notes to yourself will help you step back and gain distance from your writing. You could ask yourself questions, such as: How can I make this stronger (or clearer, or more believable)? You can include reminders, like: "Ask Mary about her experience in this area," "Check for accuracy," or "Get more information from the library."

5.9 • Keeping a Personal Reading Journal

Another good option for taking notes is a personal reading journal. This form of notetaking helps you stay interested in the material because you can relate your experiences—including your knowledge from other courses—to the reading.

How it can work:

Suppose you're doing assigned reading about eating disorders. You've heard this phrase so much that you're getting numb. The text is treating the subject in an especially dry way. You're about to fall asleep. Now, check out the cartoon to see how a personal journal could help you keep your attention focused and make connections you might otherwise miss.

How to use a personal reading journal:

- Experiment. See where the writing takes you. Use the journal to help you bring life to the reading. Feel free to create a written, audiotaped, or drawing journal.

- Date every entry (so you can see how your thinking changes).

Other things to consider:

- If you find you're writing the same kind of entry all the time, try something else. At first it might feel funny or odd, but challenge yourself.

- "Revisit" entries later. Make sure to leave extra room for later comments. (Cycling back reinforces what you've learned.)

- Don't judge or edit your original entries. Concentrate on the substance of what you're writing.

- Feel free to explore different kinds of paper, colored pens, highlighters. The more interesting you make it for yourself, the more you'll write. And the more you write, most likely, the more you'll learn and remember.

Assigning reading journals is becoming more popular among teachers. These journals can be in any subject, such as the sciences, social sciences, business, or technology. One teacher we know taught a beginning college mathematics course and had her students write a journal to help them relate to the topic in a more personal way. She was also trying to reach the students who were scared or angry about having to take the course because they felt that they never had learned to do mathematics and that they never would have to use it. One student ended up writing about very complex measurements she had to make as she was tiling her bathroom. She amazed herself as well as the other students by finding out how much she really did know about fractions. Another student wrote about how he had gone grocery shopping, went through the checkout line, put eight bags of groceries into his truck, and, just before pulling out of the parking lot, realized that his bill couldn't possibly be right. So, he carted all the bags back to the checkout line, and saved himself $50.00! Once the students saw these stories in writing, they started to reevaluate what they did know, what they were beginning to learn, and what they needed to know more about.

5.10 • Mapping

If you want to use an interesting variation in taking notes, try mapping. Maps are helpful because they capture the most important aspects of a book, article, or hand-out in a structured picture, instead of a sentence or paragraph. Mapping is fun, easy to do, and useful both in the process of constructing as well as in the act of reading.

The best way to describe a map is to show what one can look like. We've chosen "Cut It Out: Nine Myths That Have To Go" from Chapter 6.

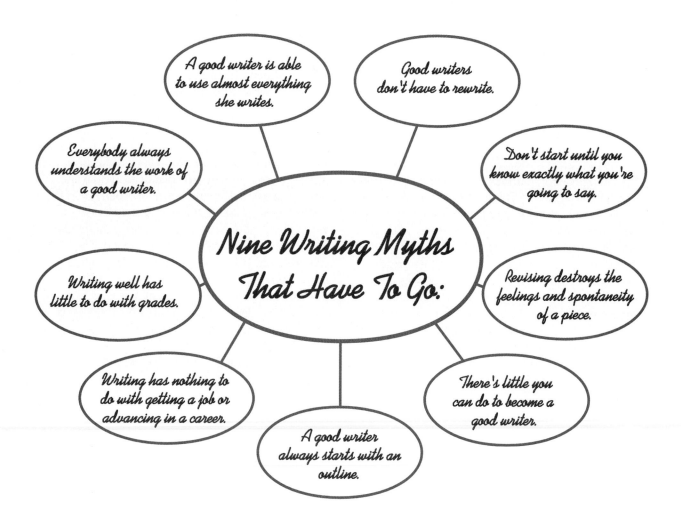

Basic tips:

1. Identify the main point. Place the main point in the center and draw a square (or other figure) around it.

2. Identify the subpoints. Place these around the main point. Draw a line between each subpoint and the main point. Draw a square (or other figure) around each subpoint.

3. For each subpoint, identify related smaller points, and locate these points below your subpoints. Draw spokes between the smaller points and each subpoint.

4. Don't worry about making an artistic map; just make one that works for you.

Mapping is effective because you interact with the text. In the process of mapping you:

- Reorganize the material you've read
- Discover connections or relationships among pieces of information in the text
- Discover connections or relationships between the text and your experiences
- Separate the most important from the least important points in the text
- Create a picture of your own understanding of the material, and, by making this picture, you can see what you're thinking

You can get as inventive as you'd like: instead of spokes, make a string of hearts, arrows, footballs, even stickers. Vary your use of color. Create wall size or small (8½ × 11) maps. Try placing your main idea in some other location.

Feel free to use mapping in combination with other techniques, such as freewriting, summarizing, and other forms of notetaking.

Experiment with mapping by yourself, with one other person, or in a group.

Other uses for mapping: "read" your own papers, take notes, find a topic, plan a speech, prepare for an exam, tackle a big project (academic or not).

5.11 • Creating and Understanding Charts

When two or more subjects (countries, business practices, art forms, diseases, time periods, experiments, laws, companies, accounting methods, etc.) are being discussed, the text can become so saturated with facts that it is tricky to follow. Sometimes the best way to understand this kind of material is by condensing it into chart form. Charts are especially valuable because, in a small space, they highlight the differences and similarities among items. The best way to explain chart making is to show you one. Following is a chart of some of the reading methods in this chapter.

How to set up the chart:

- Select the items you are comparing. For this chart we decided to select mapping, summarizing, surveying the text, and making marginal notes.

- Next, decide how you will compare the items. We chose to look at why the method is used, what the method looks like on paper, steps, application, and benefits.

	MAPPING	SUMMARIZING	SURVEYING	MARGINAL NOTES
Why	Captures information in a picture	Synthesizes much information into manageable chunk	Orients reader to text	Allows reader to connect to material
What it looks like on paper	Clustered circles and spokes	One or more paragraphs (up to about 1/4 of the length of original passage)	Not relevant	Comments, questions, words, drawings, symbols in book margins
Steps	• Read text • Identify main point • Center main point • Identify and place subpoints • Draw spokes between main and subpoints, etc.	• Survey text • Identify main points of each section • Write summary • Revise as needed	• Read title, summary, introduction, objectives, or outline • Read first paragraph under each subheading	• Start reading • Make connections • Use margins as needed
Applications	• For individuals, pairs, or groups • Works well with other reading strategies • Can use different colors, symbols, and types of paper	• For individuals, pairs, or small groups • Works well with reading log • Can be used to understand class presentations and conversations	• For individuals, pairs, or small groups • Generally quick	• Any reactions are appropriate • Can include summaries, small maps, personal and academic responses
When to use	After reading a passage	After reading a paragraph, section, or chapter	Before plunging into reading	Before, during, or after reading a passage
Benefits	• Aids memory • Condenses information • Appeals to visual learners • Helps in test preparation • Keeps reader involved • Aids comprehension	• Aids memory • Test preparation strategy • Helpful for understanding articles • Helpful for revising papers	Keeps reader involved	• Especially helpful for controversial material • Helps reader understand author's motivation • Helps reader bring in more of her own experiences • Aids memory • Helps track reading • Keeps reader focused

Once you've created your own charts, you will be able to read the charts of others much more easily. (Charts are quite common in science, history, lab, and business courses.) When you first look at a chart, get a good orientation by asking yourself two questions: *What* is being compared? And *How* are these items being compared? To understand confusing charts, rewrite them in sentence form or map them.

• Activity 5.1

Read one of the text chapters you've been assigned from another class. Review "Using the Margins" and try writing notes on the margins of your text pages. After you have finished, answer these questions:

- What kinds of comments did you make?

- Why did you make them?

- In what ways did marginal commenting affect your reading?

• Activity 5.2

Create a "Mr. Question-Person" cartoon for the section "How to Begin a Reading Assignment." What is the question you would ask? Draw or describe yourself as one of the characters interviewed. What is your response to the question? If you're feeling ambitious, add three other characters to your cartoon and describe their responses.

6

Become a More Effective (and Less Stressed-Out) Writer

Writing is one of our most complex forms of communication. By learning to do it well, you will heighten your ability to question, analyze, express, and argue your thoughts, convictions, and experiences.

The purpose of this chapter is for you to:

- Encounter some truths and debunk some common myths about writing
- Gain a clearer sense of writing as a dynamic process
- Learn special techniques for getting started and keeping ideas flowing
- Develop strategies for organizing, revising, and creating the best finished product possible
- Deal more effectively with writer's block
- Determine how to analyze and communicate with your audience
- Understand how to organize and maintain writing groups that work

6.1 • How To Think about Writing

Learning to be a good writer is one of the most rewarding experiences of college. Being a good writer will help you throughout your life. Right now you might love writing or you might hate it. No matter what your relationship, you'll discover that nearly everyone who writes faces these four truths:

1. Writing is hard. It just is.

We wish we could tell you differently. We wish we had some sort of secret that would magically make writing effortless, but we don't. Good writing is hard work. *Every* writer goes through the struggle, regardless of how easy it might look from the outside. Becoming a good writer takes a lot of effort, but the payoff is worth it.

2. Writing = making choices.

Whether you are given the topic and format or whether you have free reign, you have lots of choices to make. You have to choose every word you write. And for every word you include, you are choosing to exclude other words. In writing you must also choose what and how many details to include, how much of your own opinion to reveal (or not to reveal), how to order the information, where to place your emphasis and focus, how much research to do (if any). Everything you write will present its own challenges, and for each challenge you must choose a solution. One of the biggest challenges is to find a way to make the writing satisfying to you and something you are proud of.

3. Every piece of writing is a work in progress.

Most writers realize that a piece of writing is never really finished. When you write, you are constantly working to figure out what you want to say, drafting your ideas, then rewriting and editing. But, even as you edit, you continue to discover other things to say, how to organize your ideas more effectively, and how to appeal to your audience in a more powerful way. Sometimes you stop because you've run out of time or because another assignment is pressing. Remember, what you've learned in this process will help you the next time you start to write.

4. Writing takes many forms.

Throughout your college career you will be assigned many kinds of writing. Depending on your courses and major, you might be doing research papers, essays, fiction, lab reports, business reports, client progress notes or records, minutes of meetings, proposals, directions, advertisements, case statements, descriptions, problem statements, memos, and letters. Each type of writing or genre has its own requirements for format, organization, vocabulary, and length. And each discipline also has its own requirements as well: A lab report in psychology might look very different than one in botany. Learning the requirements of each genre and discipline in which you're writing is part of becoming a more effective communicator.

6.2 • Cut It Out: Nine Myths That Have to Go

We all have misconceptions about the process of writing, especially about how published authors write.

Myth 1: Good writers don't rewrite. Their work is perfect the first time.
Truth: Good writers almost always rewrite and edit their work. They understand that writing is a process that needs time, attention, and effort.

Myth 2: Don't start writing until you know exactly what you're going to say.
Truth: Even if good writers think they know their purpose, through the process of writing they often discover what they really want to discuss.

Myth 3: Revising destroys the feelings and the spontaneity of a piece.
Truth: Effective revising can keep the piece vibrant and also make a writer's thoughts, feelings, ideas, and images crystal clear.

Myth 4: A person is either born with writing talent or not. There's little you can do to become a good writer.
Truth: By writing a lot and getting feedback from supportive and careful readers, students can learn to write much more effectively. Writing better is a lifelong process, even for very skilled writers.

Myth 5: A good writer always starts with an outline.
Truth: Writers use lots of strategies to start. While some use outlines, others use maps, doodles, lists, or other techniques.

Myth 6: Writing has nothing to do with getting a job or advancing in your career.
Truth: Being able to compose a good cover letter and résumé will give you a valuable edge. And the ability to write clearly is one of the most prized skills in the workplace.

Myth 7: Writing well has nothing or little do to with getting a good grade once you're out of English classes. What's important is knowing the material.
Truth: In college you are asked to write in almost all your classes. When evaluating written homework, essay tests, and papers, teachers often can't separate students' writing from their knowledge of the material. Consequently, students who pay close attention to their writing (for example, make clear distinctions, give definitions, provide appropriate background information) often can get much higher grades than those who are not as careful.

Myth 8: Everybody always understands the work of a good writer.
Truth: A good writer has to work at producing good writing. For example, she has to understand the reader's needs and how to write so they understand her message. It is also important to realize that readers can have very different reactions to the same piece. Something can get in the way for a reader that has more to do with her own life situation than with the text.

Myth 9: A good writer is able to use nearly every line, word, or image he writes.
Truth: A good writer is brave enough to throw out anything that doesn't fit.

Show, don't tell

Many kinds of writing—essays, research papers, fiction—really come alive when you demonstrate your point instead of simply stating it. In other words: show, don't tell. For example, if you want to describe a disorganized student, illustrate the way he behaves so that your reader is able to create a mental picture. Describe how his room looks, how he can never find his keys or class notes, how he often leaves for the day wearing mismatched socks. Get into the habit of using descriptive, active words. Paying attention to these details will help your writing become more lively, interesting, and compelling to your reader.

6.3 • Writing Is a Process

Think of writing as many small (and large) steps. While no one can tell you the exact number or the order of the steps you'll need for each piece you do, there are some things that we can predict.

Here Are Some Things That You May Need To Do...

When you first tackle a piece:

- Figure out what the writing assignment is asking for
- Do some background reading/thinking
- Figure out a general topic
- Organize your work space
- Eliminate unwanted noise and/or set up the right sounds for you
- Make a writing work schedule
- Jot down some notes or sketch your ideas
- Get interested in doing the assignment

After you've started:

- Write drafts
- Gather information more purposefully
- Get more ideas and rewrite
- Refine your topic
- Find someone who can give you feedback

When you're finishing:

- Read your paper aloud to see if it really makes sense and says what you want
- Check the spelling manually or use a spellchecker
- Edit and proofread
- Feel good (or uncertain or determined to do better next time)

Here are some other steps that can happen in almost any part of the cycle:

- Do background reading
- Check the assignment to make sure you're on track
- Write the introduction. Some people try to write it in the beginning; many people write it at the end. Sometimes a writer will do an introduction at the beginning of the process, and then completely rewrite it when the piece is finished
- Compose the conclusion
- Include details. Sometimes people start with very small details, and these then become part of the piece. At other times, people add details only after they've written most of the piece
- Read over what you've written
- Talk to friends about your assignment
- Get a headache: Sometimes this leads to a walk, which can lead to a great idea!

6.4 • How To Get Started

Many people get stuck in the beginning waiting for something magical to happen. Magic is nice, but don't count on it. Here are some tried and true ways to help you begin.

List and select. (This technique works especially well if you have lots of topic choices.)

1. List all the possible topics you could write about.

2. Select from this list.

3. Write a paragraph about one or two of these and see how each feels.

4. If nothing comes, choose something else from your list.

Freewrite. (This technique works well for choosing topics and for figuring out what you want to or can say once you have your topic.)
Freewriting is writing as fast as you can for a certain length of time, say ten minutes. Don't stop, and don't worry about organization, punctuation, or grammar. Just write. The purpose of freewriting is to unclog your brain, loosen up your thoughts, and stop censuring yourself. You can do a version of freewriting by recording your thoughts on cassette tape. Don't worry about rambling, repeating words, or sounding silly.

Outline or map.
An outline is a list of the major points you'll make and the order you'll use. Once you have a topic, making an outline can show you how to proceed. As you write, you can keep referring to your map or outline, and, of course, you can keep changing it. You can use standard paper, a large flip chart, or a felt board.

Read, read, read:

- The assignment question (sometimes reading this question out loud can be really helpful)

- Sample student or published papers on the topic

- The assigned reading…again

- Your notes

Talk to others and to yourself:

- Discuss the assignment with other students (those in your class and those who have previously done this type of writing).

- Explain the assignment to someone else.

Ask yourself some of these questions:

- How is this assignment similar to others I've had?

- How is it different?

- What do I like about the assignment?

- What questions do I have about the assignment?

- How can I find the answers to these questions?

Rewrite the assignment in your own words.

Allow for sudden insight:

- Always carry the assignment with you, as well as a pen and some blank paper; you never know when you'll get an idea.

- Place a pen and some blank paper by your bed; you might have dreams about the assignment!

Dance or sing your interpretation of the assignment.
Sometimes using other ways of understanding an assignment will lead you to discover approaches that you would otherwise miss. So, test out your singing voice and dust off your dancing shoes. You might be surprised how your creative instincts can contribute to your work!

6.5 • Brainstorming: A Walk on the Wild Side

Brainstorming is based on the notion that sometimes the best ideas come from unlikely connections. We can become so locked in logic that it's hard to loosen up enough to let those unlikely connections happen. Brainstorming is a group technique used to make this kind of creative thinking easier. When you brainstorm, keep two words in mind: *unrestrained* and *spontaneous*. You and your fellow brainstormers want to be both of those things and encourage the kind of freewheeling exchange of ideas that can inspire an ingenious concept or generate an excellent solution.

How to brainstorm:

- Identify the problem for which you're hoping to find a solution or idea. Examples are a topic for a project or a way for a club to raise money.

- Set a limit. Some people like time limits. Otherwise, choose something such as a specific number of ideas you'll generate before you stop.

- Make this deal with each person in your brainstorming group: No idea is too lunatic, bizarre, or far-out to be considered. Don't censor yourself or anyone else.

- Since brainstorming thrives on the widest possible range of ideas, encourage shy or reticent people to participate. One technique is to agree no one person can offer more than one idea consecutively.

- Appoint a scribe who will write down all the ideas *exactly* as they are expressed. We recommend putting the ideas on a flip chart or blackboard for everyone to see during the process. A flip chart is useful if you're going to want a permanent record of the brainstorming session. Don't cover up filled pages: Display them.

- Don't worry about spelling or grammar. Don't edit or try to 'fix' or refine anything at this point. Also, don't disregard an idea because it seems like a duplicate of one already on the board: There may be a subtle difference that will become important later.

- When you've reached the limit, review everything you've identified. Rank the ideas. Throw out the ones that everyone agrees are absurd. Keep the ones that have possibilities. If there are any that people don't understand, have the originators explain them, and rank or discard them as well.

- Have everyone vote for their favorite five ideas.

- Explore if any top-ranked ideas, or any combination of ideas, could contribute to the solution you've been looking for. You'll be surprised how often unlikely approaches can create a great inspiration.

Unleash your creativity

Even when you work alone you can tap into your creative energy. Freewriting is a form of brainstorming. As with group brainstorming, be unconstrained and spontaneous when you brainstorm alone. Writing without stopping or editing can help you override the logical side of your brain and allow you to access your intuitive abilities. To get ideas, look at artwork, read poetry, listen to music; use these and other creative influences to help you make unusual and productive connections. We all have the ability to think creatively. Whether you're working with a group or by yourself, make use of techniques that stimulate your whole brain.

6.6 • Don't Leave Your Reader at the Station

In writing, you take your reader on a journey: You go to the train station together, buy your tickets for the same destination, and get on the same train. Unfortunately, too often a writer takes the trip alone, while the reader looks for his travel partner and gets bored waiting for the journey to begin! So don't leave *your* reader at the station.

How to take your reader with you:

- Figure out who will be reading your paper. Just your teacher? Your peers? Some combination? Or does your assignment include a specific audience, such as a manager, an agency director, a client, or a customer?

- Decide how much experience your audience has with your topic. Just because your audience might be the professor doesn't mean he is an expert in this topic. In fact, sometimes you'll know more than he does on a particular issue. This is especially true of English teachers who assign a wide range of essay topics.

- Think about whether your audience has a point of view on the subject you're writing about. Is your audience neutral? Pro? Anti? Do you know why? If you don't know, think about the personality and interests of your audience and see if you can make some guesses.

- Consider what you know about your audience's preferences regarding writing style, word choice, and format. Does your audience appreciate or require more casual, informal writing that has personal examples, stories, descriptions? Or does your audience prefer more formal writing?

- If you don't really know the answers to these questions, sharpen your observations of your audience. If your teacher is your audience, the next time you're in class notice if your teacher tells jokes or stories; if he does, he might be more likely to appreciate these techniques in your writing. Check to see how formal your teacher's class presentations are. If your teacher is very structured and rigorous, he may respond well to a very precise paper. If you still don't have a clear enough picture of your professor, imagine yourself having a conversation with him and talk yourself through the writing.

Take action:

1. Use everything you now know about your audience to help you write and revise your writing.

2. If your reader is unfamiliar with your topic, make sure to present information carefully and in as organized a way as necessary. You might need to provide additional background information, define all your terms, and give examples so your reader can follow you. If your audience is unfamiliar with your topic, you will teach through your writing. (It's safer to assume your readers are unfamiliar with a topic if you have no way to check their knowledge.)

3. Ask yourself, "What do I want my audience to know, do, think, and/or feel as a result of reading this piece?" Make a list. After you have written the first draft of your paper, reread this list. Make sure the list and your draft match. If not, revise your draft or reconsider what's on your list.

How to Use Your Knowledge of Audience to Help You Write Essays

WHAT I KNOW ABOUT MY AUDIENCE	HOW I CAN USE THIS INFORMATION
Knows a lot about topic	• Minimize background information.
	• Get to points quickly.
	• Try to provide some fresh material about topic to avoid boring reader.
	• Provide fresh perspective.
Opposes my point of view	• Lead into my point of view slowly.
	• Give background information from credible sources that clearly support my point of view.
	• Show I understand the opposing viewpoint.
	• Be realistic about what I want audience to know, think, or do as a result of reading my paper.
	• Write final paragraphs that reinforce purpose.
Knows little about topic	• Paper must serve as teaching tool.
	• Go step by step.
	• Define all terms.
	• Use frequent examples.
	• Build bridges between sections.
	• Provide introduction that forecasts topics.
	• Use subheads where possible.
	• Ending should summarize.
	• If a long paper, each section could have its own summary.

6.7 • Organizing Your Work

Every piece of writing has to have some sort of organization (unless you are writing an unstructured journal entry or a personal, free-flow note). To organize your writing, you'll want to figure out how your paper begins, how it ends, and what goes in between. Then you need to determine how to arrange these pieces.

Considering these three questions can help you organize your writing:

1. What are the basic points you're trying to make? You can find out what your main points are in two ways: Make a list of the points you want to make before you start writing; or finish your first draft, read it, and pull out your basic points from what you've written.

2. Can you rate your basic points in their order of importance? For example, if you're writing about the consequences of suntanning, you might decide to cover the cost of suncare products, the fact that too much sun often causes premature skin aging, and the increased risk of skin cancer, including the deadly melanoma. Obviously, these three results are not equally significant. How would you rate them—from most to least important? These kinds of decisions can help you order the information in your paper.

3. Now that you have an idea about how your points relate to one another in importance, how can this information help you decide on your organization? You might decide to start with the most important point and end up with the least important. You might decide to end your paper with the most important point. The kind of writing you've been assigned, and what you know about your audience, can help you determine the best order for your information.

Effective Opening and Closing Paragraphs

For essay and many kinds of research writing, your answers to the previous questions will help you craft an opening and closing paragraph in a way that satisfies your reader.

Opening Paragraphs

The first paragraph (or paragraphs) can introduce the topic, present the order of the information in your paper, or provide background information. Mostly, you'll want to use the opening paragraph(s) to grab your reader's attention, give an idea of what your piece is about, and intrigue your reader. Devices include startling statistics or facts, questions, quotations, stories, scenes, or descriptions.

If you're writing a paper about the causes of teenage suicide, your opening paragraph might describe a suicidal 16-year-old who is depressed and feeling hopeless because of school and boyfriend trouble. A strong and vivid opening paragraph gives your reader a reason to care about your topic.

Closing Paragraphs

One effective way to conclude a paper is to ask yourself this question: What do I want my reader to know, do, think or feel as a result of reading this work?

Suppose your paper is on recycling and your main point is that each individual's efforts matter. After reading your paper, you want your audience to hesitate before throwing that aluminum can away. Your ending paragraphs might reinforce a few of the statistics you've already cited and make a few pointed remarks, such as "So, the next time you're about to throw away that aluminum can, think about all those ugly landfills and resist the temptation. Be part of the solution, not the problem." Your closing paragraphs reinforce your message, so consider them carefully.

6.8 • No Guts, No Glory: Rough Drafts and Final Drafts

Last week you wrote a pretty good paper: right length, grammatically correct, impressive words. But your professor's written notes indicate that he thinks the paper isn't complete, and, in fact, it's more like a rough draft than a final paper. Angry and frustrated, you ball up your masterpiece and throw it away. Later, when you retrieve it, you reread his comments and grudgingly begin to see his side of things.

Here's a hard-to-accept message: When you're in the thick of writing, it might be impossible to know whether you've got a final paper or a rough draft. You have to be willing to look honestly at your writing, consider the differences between rough and final drafts, and make the changes you need to finish.

First, know the difference between rough and final drafts.

A rough draft is often:

- Sketchy, at least in some areas, or superficial
- Rambling or stream of consciousness writing
- Missing one or more parts (in essay writing this could mean an introduction or a conclusion)
- Inconsistent (for example, formal in one part and informal in another)
- Written with imprecise words or phrases (such as "things" or "lots of")
- Disorganized, repetitive, circular; essential information might be omitted; information might seem out of order
- Perceived by others to be in a "code" they can't decipher
- Okay as far as it goes, but stops short of making the points you want

A final draft is often:

- Concise and to the point
- Well-organized
- Consistent in style
- Complete in its information
- Interesting and clear to the reader

Use time–tested strategies to figure out how to take your rough draft and make it into a final draft:

- Read your paper out loud or have someone read it to you.
- Put it away for a few hours at least, and preferably for a few days. Then look at it again through this (hopefully) fresh lens.
- Get feedback on your paper from a tutor, a teacher, your advisor.
- Read sample student papers.

The harder you've worked, the more you risk "falling in love" with a piece and losing perspective. (The solution, however, is not to work less hard, because you'll just end up handing in a rough draft that is uninteresting to you *and* your reader.) Some signs of falling in love with your writing:

- You're furious over the feedback you've gotten.
- You feel a compulsive parental urge to protect your "baby" from critical eyes.
- You're absolutely sure no one in the entire world, in any century, has ever thought of what you've just written.
- You're convinced you'll get the Pulitzer Prize.
- You think your work is perfect.

 **HOT TIP!**

*Remember, love is for friends, significant others, parents, children, animals, and the earth. Don't **love** your writing; instead, develop an attitude of enlightened respect, which will let you appreciate your own work and still be able to improve it.*

6.9 • Revising Smart, Revising with Heart

Revising might not always be a peak experience, but it doesn't have to be a night-mare either. To help you stay sane and productive, you'll need to understand what revising is and what it isn't, how you can sidetrack yourself, and what you can do to get back on track.

Revising *is*:

- Recrafting your rough draft and making it clearer and more interesting to your reader as well as more responsive to the assignment
- Working with the content and organization—you know, the **big stuff**, not just changing a word or a line
- Having the courage to change something when you realize it isn't working. This might mean deleting your favorite line, image, or paragraph
- Seeing your piece anew, not just as the person whose sweat poured into this project, but as the reader who needs to understand what's being communicated

Revising is *not*:

- The same as editing. Editing only deals with the simpler stuff such as spelling, tenses, punctuation, and word repetition.
- A formula. When you revise, you become an explorer, finding your own way with each writing assignment.

Ways you can become sidetracked:

- You have unrealistic goals:

  You want to be perfect or brilliant, or get the highest grade that anyone has ever gotten on the assignment. Or maybe you want to write as well as some other student whose work you admire. The trouble is that when you have those goals, it's too easy to focus on what's not in your control. (Remember: There's no such thing as the perfect piece, and your writing will never be just like someone else's. You have your own unique gifts and sensibilities.)

- Your strategies are backfiring:

  Micro mania: Maybe you're getting too caught up in the small details, such as spending an entire evening finding that ideal word that starts with a w and has sixteen letters.
  Time mismanagement: You spend most of your time researching and writing your first draft, only to realize you have too little time to revise.
  Inadequate information: You don't have enough information, don't understand the assignment, or are not sure how to interpret the article you're writing about. First you write A and then you rewrite it as B, then as C, but you have no basis for deciding which is better.
  Self-blaming: As you're revising, you keep telling yourself that the piece is lousy anyway and you're just wasting your time. Even when you come up with a solution for, say, an introduction that works well, you think, "it should have taken me less time," or "anyone could have come up with that."

Self-exile: You don't have a good sense of what your professor expects. Maybe you keep re-working what you've done to make it longer, more comprehensive, and graphically magnificent. In reality, your work might far exceed what's expected (or, maybe not). As you continue, you grow more and more uncomfortable because you don't know what's enough, what's too much, and how to put the information together.

Ways to Get Yourself Back on Track

PROBLEM	SOLUTION
Micro–mania	• Highlight smaller problem areas, such as finding better words; return only if you have time.
	• Prioritize what you need to do and start revising the BIG STUFF first.
Time Mismanagement	• Make a plan for the entire writing project.
	• Give yourself at least two days to revise, more for bigger projects.
Insufficient Information	• Get feedback from teachers, tutors.
	• Reread the assignment.
	• Read sample student papers.
	• Step back and develop real criteria for making choices.
Self–blaming	• Restrain yourself.
	• Find three good points about your piece.
	• Develop an overall plan for writing improvement and use each assignment to advance toward your goal.
	• Learn to appreciate your progress.
Self–exile	• Get feedback.
	• Read sample papers.
	• Read related materials.
	• Talk to your professor.
Unrealistic Goals	• Focus on your personal best.
	• Make a few achievable goals.

6.10 • Writing Is Graphic, Too

Writing and reading are more than mental endeavors; they involve using our eyes as well. By learning to incorporate some simple graphic design techniques, you can make your writing look a lot more professional and appealing to your reader. (Check the example to see how all these elements work together.)

White Space

This term refers to the amount of space you put between paragraphs and sections and the size you choose for margins. If your piece is packed together in one continuous clump of information, with no breaks and narrow margins, it might seem dense and overwhelming to your reader. Make sure your margins are generous (at least one inch on the sides and maybe a bit larger for top and bottom). Put spaces between paragraphs and sections. Good use of white space can make your writing much easier on the eye, as well as more inviting and accessible to your audience.

Fonts

A font is a style of type. Fonts come in a variety of sizes, and almost all have variations. Most fonts are divided into two categories: *serif* (letters with little tails, like Times Roman) and *sans serif* (letters without tails, like **Arial**). Most word processing systems offer you a range of fonts. For academic writing, it's generally best to use a serif font (it's easier to read) in 11 point or 12 point size. You might make your headings a different font, a sans serif font for example, and use 13 point or 14 point size, as a way to distinguish them from the rest of the text.

Bold, *italic*, CAPS, SMALL CAPS, and <u>underline</u>

These are font variations: ways to make fonts look different without changing their basic style. Use these features to emphasize words or points, set something apart from the rest of the text, indicate a new term or foreign word, and compile your bibliography and references.

Heads

Heads are titles—words, phrases, short sentences, or questions—you can use to label major sections of your paper. Heads suggest what's coming next and forecast information you will present. These are really useful in giving your reader a preview of the order and main points of your paper. They also can keep you organized. *Subheads* label section parts. In this book we have used both heads and subheads. It's best to distinguish heads and subheads from your text and from each other. Here are some ways to do this:

- Make heads and subheads bold.
- Center heads on the page.
- Make the heads a point size larger than the text; keep subheads the same size as the text.
- Underline the subheads or place them at the left margin.

Bullets

Bullets allow you to present information concisely. We've used this technique extensively in this text. Look at the previous section for an example of bullets. Most word processing programs offer standard bullets (which look like filled circles) in a variety of sizes, as well as a range of other shapes (stars, diamonds, arrows) from which to choose.

Rules

Graphic designers call lines "rules." These are lines that you can place over or under text, use to separate sections in a paper, or include as a decorative element. Rules are not the same as underlines. To create and use rules, you will need to find out how your word processing or desktop publishing system does them.

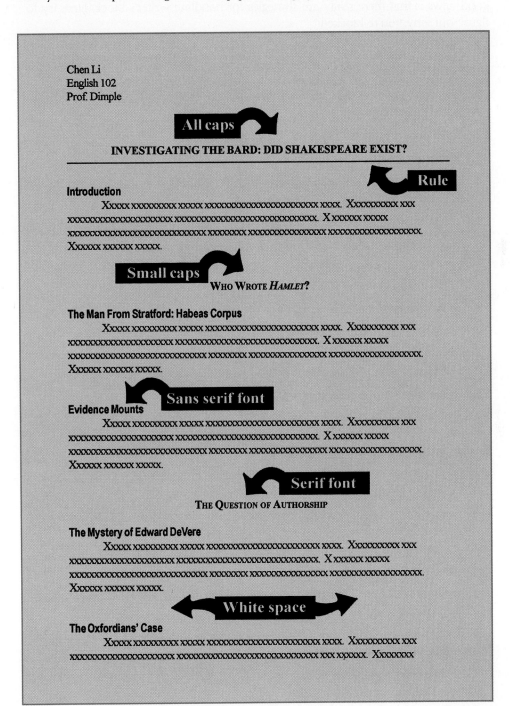

6.11 • Counter That Block

Imagine you're sitting in front of a blank screen or paper. Nothing, absolutely nothing, comes. Hours crawl by, and you have produced not one shred of material. The good news is that there really are strategies for handling writer's block. First, try to figure out why you're blocked.

Twelve reasons for writer's block (these can happen by themselves or in any combination):

1. You don't have enough information about the topic, your audience, or the genre in which you're writing.

2. You have so much to say that you're overwhelmed.

3. You're overcensoring yourself.

4. You expect your writing to be perfect: You are afraid that if it's not perfect, you have failed as a writer.

5. You're expecting too much, too soon.

6. You don't understand the issues that you're writing about.

7. You're torn between telling your reader what you think he wants to hear and telling what you need to say.

8. You're exhausted or ill.

9. Something else going on in your life (with family, friends, finances, for example) needs your attention.

10. The topic you're writing about is too painful for you right now.

11. You're angry at the professor who assigned this paper.

12. Add any others.

Some things you can try to fight writer's block:

- If you have too much information, are overcensoring, or dealing with a sensitive topic, freewrite your ideas so you can see them.

- Get more information. Read something more on the topic. Read sample papers on the same assignment.

- Go to the tutoring center. Discuss approaches you could take. Talk with your professor and your classmates. Use a tape recorder and talk out loud to yourself.

- If personal issues are getting in the way, consider talking with a counselor, a trusted friend, or an advisor.

- If the paper is too painful or raises issues that are unresolved for you, consider changing your topic or reframing it.

- Get some exercise. Change your activity. Come back to the writing later with a clearer mind.

- Use a tape recorder or write yourself a letter explaining why you're having a hard time.

- Write a dialogue between yourself and any negative people in your head.
- Approach the topic from a new angle:

   Draw your ideas.

   Create a map.

   Doodle.

   Make a cartoon.

   Write a dramatic description of yourself trying to write.

- Invite a friend to do her work in the same room with you. (Sometimes just quiet company is enough to get you started.)
- Bargain with yourself: Tackle a tiny piece of the assignment and then give yourself a reward!

HOT TIP!

Sometimes the things that get in your way are very useful. For example, having a lot to say is wonderful. Just find a way to get your ideas out before they disappear and then select the most appropriate ones. High expectations will serve you well when you learn to use them to motivate instead of squash you. Remember, most writers have a block at some time. The trick is to recognize **your** *block and find your way out.*

6.12 • Making Writing Groups Work

Most writing is communication: You are trying to express something—an idea, an argument, an experience—so that whoever reads your work understands it in the way you intend. Working with a writing group can give you insight into how others react to your writing. Also, becoming an effective critic of other people's writing will help you develop your own.

A sample scenario:

Four people comprise this group: Russ, Tyrone, Akita, and Simone.

1. Akita is leader for this session. She lets everyone know how much time is available to each person. (Divide the time available by the number of people in the group.) She will watch the time carefully and indicate when it's time to move on to the next person.

2. Akita asks who would like to go first. Russ volunteers.

3. Russ reads his piece aloud while the group listens.

4. Russ reads his piece aloud again. This time group members take notes.

5. One by one, Tyrone, Simone, and Akita tell Russ how they responded to his piece. They describe what worked for them and what didn't work so well. They also make specific suggestions. Russ listens and takes notes.

6. When everyone has finished responding, Russ asks questions of individual group members about their comments.

7. Russ thanks everyone for the feedback. Akita checks the time and asks who would like to go next. Simone responds, and the process begins again.

Tips for effective critiquing:

- Always be constructive.

- Make your comments—about what worked for you and what didn't—as concrete, specific, and detailed as possible.

- If you have feedback that would mean substantial rewriting of the piece, ask the writer's permission.

- Indicate by your body language and tone of voice that you respect the writer and understand how vulnerable it can feel to have your work reviewed.

- Separate the work from the writer. You might say, "This sentence seems to describe…" rather than "*You* don't really believe that, do you?"

Tips for asking for and listening to the feedback from others:

- Try to be as clear as you can about the kind of feedback you'd like. For example, in an early draft you might want the group to concentrate only on whether the idea for your paper makes sense. Later, you might want feedback on how effectively you've answered the assignment question and how clearly you've written.

- Remember, unless you're showing a finished paper, you'll want a balance of positive comments along with specific remarks about what is not working.

- If you're feeling overwhelmed by the amount of feedback you've gotten, you should not keep getting more. You won't hear the feedback, or you'll hear it out of context. Feel free to stop the process at any point.

- Don't be afraid to ask for more positive comments. We all need appreciation!

Tips for creating effective groups:

- Select people who are committed to giving honest but constructive feedback and who want to work on their own writing.

- Designate a leader to keep track of the time, keep everyone focused, and intervene if someone is making negative or unconstructive remarks. The role of leader can rotate among group members from meeting to meeting.

- Pay attention to your own learning style, as well as the styles of others. For example, do you need to see as well as hear the writing? Make adjustments so that everyone can function effectively.

6.13 • Using Sample Papers

One of the best ways of understanding your professor's expectations for papers (or exams) is to look at either student work from past classes or published work on a similar kind of assignment. The goal is not to clone your paper but to get ideas for presenting information and organizing your own topic. As you analyze sample student material, you'll discover your professor's preferences for word choice, format, graphics, and attention-grabbing techniques.

Guidelines for using sample student papers

Obtaining student papers:

- Ask your professor for sample student work. Three or four papers are best. Looking at sample student papers is not cheating.

- Try to obtain the original assignment; professors frequently change assignments (even a slight alteration could have an impact on what students have written).

- Clarify whether the instructor is giving you models (highly regarded or complete) or papers that need additional work. You can learn from both.

- Ask for papers with faculty comments, as these can be especially helpful.

Obtaining published papers:

- Consult your textbook for samples.

- Ask your professor, your school's reference librarian, or a staff person at the tutoring or writing center to recommend books, professional journals, or other sources that have sample papers of the type you'll need to write.

Working with the Papers

Questions you can ask yourself about the treatment of the topic:

- How much and what kinds of information does the writer use to address each part of the assignment?

- Is each part easy to find, or do you have to work at "fishing" it out?

- What kinds of words, terms, and concepts does the writer use? Does she define new terms clearly?

- What other techniques (examples, quotations, stories, humor, descriptions) does the writer use to make the piece appealing and convincing to the audience or responsive to the assignment?

Questions you can ask yourself about organization:

- What is the order of the information the writer uses?

- As the writer finishes one part of the assignment and starts another, does he alert the reader? If so, how? How does the writer move from one section or point to another?

- If there is an introduction, what kind of information does it contain?

- If there is an ending section, what purpose does it serve?

- How is the paper formatted? Are there heads? Subheads? Large or small margins? What graphics elements are used?

Applying your personal reactions:

- On the whole, how clear is this paper in relation to the original assignment?
- How effective is the organization? How has the writer organized it?
- Are there any places that confuse you? Why?
- What are the paper's strongest areas? What are the weakest?
- How effective is the formatting?
- How careful is the writer to define all terms?
- Do faculty comments reveal any preferences about organization, topic choice, and formatting?
- Applying what you learned, what ideas do you have for your own paper?

When you're developing your own work, read your paper as if it were someone else's. Step back and analyze your work using some of the previous questions.

Hey, it's Mr. Question-Person !

Each week Mr. Question-Person roams the campus armed with only a notebook and camera, seeking answers to today's hard student questions. He strikes without warning, so watch out: maybe this week you'll find yourself in Mr. Question-Person!

This week's question: *Do you find sample papers useful?*

Skip G. & Shalimar L.
Majors: Bus Adm & Adolesc Psy

"They really help us manage and develop our own work. Sometimes we wish they offered sample relationships."

Khan An N.
Major: Electrical Engineering

"I especially like the ones that are lively and well constructed. I can really connect with what they're trying to do."

Nathan J.
Major: Computer Science

"When I analyze someone else's work, I like to compute the different ways they make their points and give them a score. I usually win."

Mercedes R.
Major: Drama

"One paper I read was so good I found out who the author was and got her autograph!"

6.14 • Two Checklists: Questions To Keep in Mind as You Write and Before You Turn in Your Paper

Questions to answer in the early stages of writing:

- What is the assignment? Can I summarize it in one sentence? (If not, you might want to go back and reread the instructions.)
- What do I already know about the topic of the assignment?
- Who is my audience? What does the audience already know about this subject? What background information do I need to provide so I don't lose the audience?
- What are the three to five most important points I want to make?
- How might an audience challenge some of my points? How can I make my points more convincing?
- What might be the best way to organize this piece? How can I put it together so it makes sense?
- What do I want my reader to *know, think, feel,* or *do* as a result of reading this piece?

Questions to answer before turning in your paper:

- Have I revised my piece at least once?
- Is each part of the assignment addressed completely?
- Is each part easy to follow?
- Is my piece clearly organized?
- Have I incorporated graphic design details when appropriate?
- Can I say in one sentence the main point of my piece? (If not, you're probably not done yet!)
- Is my opening paragraph compelling (if appropriate to the writing assignment)?
- Is my closing paragraph strong and clear (if appropriate to the writing assignment)?
- Have I "shown, not told" whenever possible (if appropriate to the writing assignment)?
- Have I checked my paper for typos and grammatical errors?
- Have I run spellchecker or manually checked the spelling?
- Are the pages numbered, in consecutive order, and is my name on the front cover?
- Have I stapled my paper or otherwise secured the pages?

• Activity 6.1

Select one of the writing myths, or make up one of your own. In two paragraphs talk about how this myth applies to you.

• Activity 6.2

Think back to an occasion when you had to really struggle to begin a paper or project. Now look at the cartoon in "How to Get Started." Instead of Skip's character, draw yourself. Create as many frames you'd like and change the text in whatever way reflects your experience. If you prefer, simply write about what the process was like for you.

7

The Art of Handling Big and Small Projects

Projects are assignments that combine several parts (such as research, writing, and presentation), sometimes involve a group, and usually require a substantial period of time to complete. Successfully completing a project means learning how to juggle all the pieces.

The purpose of this chapter is for you to:

- Develop strategies to analyze what it takes (time, energy, special knowledge, collaboration) to complete a big assignment
- Learn how to schedule the many parts of a project
- Determine the best ways to manage and monitor work on the project
- Consider criteria for joining a study/project group
- Become familiar with ground rules for group maintenance and success

7.1 • Understanding the Assignment

You've just started a project and already you're lost. Or, maybe you've been working on a project for a while, but you're not making much headway. Are you sure you understand it?

Some ways to understand your project's instructions:

- Read the instructions over as many times as you need to, silently and/or out loud.
- Underline, highlight, or circle key words or phrases. Make sure you understand them.
- Figure out how many parts or steps the project has. Number them.
- Rewrite the assignment instructions in your own words.
- If the assignment is not making sense, consult your class notes or text.
- Put the project away for a while and return to it later. If it is still not clear, contact the professor, another student in the same course, or the tutoring center.

If you decide to contact the professor to go over the assignment, but are feeling a little (or a lot) embarrassed, do this: Describe all the steps you've taken and the time you've already put into the process. Our confession to you: Sometimes a student's question helps instructors see just how confusing an assignment actually is!

Examples of projects:

- Books or lots of handouts to read
- Research paper
- Videotaped presentation
- Series of interviews and a report of what you found
- Writing lesson plans for a class you'll teach
- Studying for a big test
- In-class presentation involving research and audiovisuals
- Campus event you organize
- Newsletter you help produce
- Portfolio of your work
- Art show you mount

7.2 • Scheduling for Success

You don't have to wait until you have a large block of time available to complete a project. In fact, projects requiring more than two hours should probably be cut into smaller, more manageable pieces.

Avoid being overwhelmed by the time a project will take:

- Imagine each project and paper (and maybe even shorter homework assignments) as a series of tasks or steps.

- Try listing all the steps you'll need to do.

- Estimate the amount of time you need to complete each step.

- Decide on the order of the steps, if that's important.

- Plan when you'll do each step. Be as specific as possible in your planning ("2 P.M. tomorrow" is better than "in the afternoon").

- Consult your calendar to make sure you won't have a conflict.

- Check off each step as you go along.

- Adjust your plan as necessary.

Anatomy of a small project

"Read pages 1–16 from Chapter 1: "Personal Conflict Resolution Styles." Then, using an example from your life, describe in one or more typed pages a conflict and how you attempted to resolve it."

We suggest this possible plan. (Remember, everyone is different. The number of steps and the amount of time needed for each step will vary from person to person.)

1. Reread the assignment instructions (5 minutes or less).

2. Read pages 1–16 (1 hour).

3. Take notes on the text, go back and highlight, and/or make notes in the margin (30 minutes).

4. Think about times you've had conflicts (10 minutes).

5. Select a time you would be willing to write about (5 minutes).

6. Make an outline, map, picture, list, and/or doodle about your conflict experience (10 minutes).

7. Write or type a rough draft (one hour).

8. Revise as much as you need to (30 minutes each time).

9. When you're satisfied with the content of your paper, edit for spelling, grammar, and punctuation (30 minutes).

10. Make two copies: one for your file, and one to turn in (10 minutes).

Approximate time: 4–5 hours

7.3 • Keeping Track of Your Project

Because they take more time and involve more steps than daily homework assignments, projects can be more challenging. One of the biggest challenges is keeping track of which parts you've completed and which you need to finish. Keep track of your progress so you have the time you need for the whole project, and you don't miss your deadlines. It's also easier to forget about a project, especially if it's not due until late in the semester and your professor doesn't keep reminding the class.

With bigger projects you might:

- Have more time management challenges
- Lose some of your work
- Get sidetracked
- Lose interest or feel overwhelmed
- Need to learn new skills (research, interviewing, computer work), which takes additional time and energy. Don't forget to schedule time for learning these skills.

Strategies for keeping yourself motivated:

Take the time you need to find a topic you can live with and want to learn about. Find a way to relate the project to your life, another class, or your career. You'll be working on this project for a while.

Ask yourself:

- What's the one thing I like about this project so far?
- How can I apply this project to my major (or, how is this project helping me choose a major)?
- What skills am I learning?
- What information am I learning?
- What am I learning about myself?

Strategies for keeping yourself organized:

- Keep your project materials in one place that is off-limits to everyone else.
- As you start to work, create a separate pile for each part of your project. Use different colored paper for each different section. Label your piles (these change as you go along). Date everything.
- At the end of each of your work sessions, write yourself a brief note about what you did and what you'll do next.
- Monitor your progress. For example, make a large visual wall chart so you can track your work.

Don't isolate yourself. Consider joining (or creating) a student group where you can talk about your project and get feedback on how you're doing. If you're not in a project group, from time to time get feedback from your professor or others on how you're doing.

Hey, it's Mr. Question-Person !

Each week Mr. Question-Person roams the campus armed with only a notebook and camera, seeking answers to today's hard student questions. He strikes without warning, so watch out: maybe this week you'll find yourself in Mr. Question-Person!

This week's question: **What methods do you use to manage your projects?**

Sylvia Q.
Major:
Psychology

"I worry a lot, so I make a schedule and check it <u>all the time</u>. Not that I'm compulsive or anything."

Phyllis P.
Major:
Economics

"Whenever I have a large project, I make a chart so that I can track all the pieces. Especially good is red construction paper."

Nathan J.
Major:
Computer
Science

"I wrote a subroutine that allows me instant access to all aspects of my data. Would you like to see it?"

Bruno R.
Major:
Physical Ed.

"I don't have time to manage my project because it's already overdue, and I'm late for practice."

7.4 • Understanding Project Cycles

You've been assigned a big project. You notice that your emotions fluctuate quite a bit about your topic, about the process of doing the project, and about your belief in your ability. This is all quite natural.

The highs and lows of life on the project:

- You may have moments of intense enthusiasm about your topic.

- You may flounder at times or get completely lost.

- You think you understand what you're doing, and then your understanding slips away.

- You may feel lots of pressure, which decreases your motivation to turn in quality work.

- At times you may not see much progress, even when you've actually made some.

- At times you may feel like it's all coming together.

- Just before the end you may feel the most discouraged.

- At the end you may be relieved or feel let down.

Adopt a trial–and–error approach:

When one method doesn't work, keep trying new approaches. Don't get so locked into something that you can't give it up when you need to. Remember that even a very small adjustment can make a big difference.

Should you change your topic once you start?

Many times students think about giving up on their topics at the first sign of difficulty. But before you bail out, it's a good idea to analyze what the problem actually is; otherwise, it could just follow you into the next topic choice. Reevaluate by considering some of these questions on your topic choice:

- Did you choose a topic that's too broad to handle? Too technical? Too complex?
- Are your challenges more about managing the project than about the specific topic?

- If you change your topic now, will you have enough time to develop the new project?
- Are other people involved? If so, how will they feel about this switch?
- Is it possible that your original topic will work if you modify it? If it's too broad, could you find ways to narrow your focus? If the topic is too narrow, could you broaden it? If it seems dull, could you step back, find the interesting parts, and then expand those?

7.5 • Pros and Cons of Joining a Study Group

A study or project group is composed of two or more people who gather together, usually on a regular basis, to share ideas, learn the course material, and give each other support. Some students feel they couldn't survive college without study groups; some students don't use them. And for many students, joining a study group is necessary at least once in a while.

Advantages:

- You won't have to study alone. Groups can make studying more personal and comfortable, and less isolating.

- They're a great way to meet new people; for those group members you already know, a shared group experience adds a new dimension to your relationship.

- You get lots of ideas and perspectives.

- You have the opportunity to learn others' favorite study, writing, time, and stress management techniques.

- You can help each other clarify assignments.

- You motivate each other. It can be easier to do the work because you know others are counting on you to be prepared.

- Being in the group reinforces material because you're explaining, demonstrating, and summarizing for each other.

- You can try out your ideas—and get feedback on them—before going to class or taking an exam.

- You can distribute the work instead of necessarily doing it all, or doing it all at the deepest level. (We do recommend you read all required text passages, however.)

- Participating in a study group is empowering in several ways: You are taking control of your study environment. You are learning some of the skills of teamwork. You are also learning how to look at issues from several points of view.

Before you join, you might want to consider these factors:

- You may feel uncomfortable in groups and prefer to study alone.

- It takes time to set up a group, especially in the beginning. Once the group is running, it's another time commitment.

- It might be hard to find a place and time that fits all members' schedules.

- You have to work at establishing a system or format for organizing the meeting; otherwise, the group can veer off track.

- If everyone is not equally committed, some may do more work than others.

- If someone is unprepared, the group might spend too much time bringing that person along.

- At times, the variety of people and ideas may get overwhelming.

- A group member can feel "upstaged" by others who insist on showing off their knowledge.

- If you're unprepared, you may feel embarrassed or uncomfortable.

Would you benefit from a study group? Here are some questions to ask:

- What do you like least about studying or working on a project alone? What do you like best?
- What do you like least about studying in a group? What do you like best?
- What do you expect from a study group?
- What can you contribute to this group? If you already know who some of the members will be, consider what each of them can contribute.
- Do you have the time (two hours/week or whatever the group has scheduled)?

- Can you get to the group meeting on time and stay through to the end?
- How hard or easy is it for you to focus on academics in a group? (If staying on track is hard for you, it doesn't mean you shouldn't participate. But do discuss how the group will keep itself organized so that it can stick to its agenda.)

7.6 • How To Run a Group Session

Study groups are most effective when the members follow some ground rules and are sensitive to group dynamics.

Basic Ground Rules

Membership:

- Select the right number of people for your group. (Six to eight committed people is a good number; the more people, the longer each session probably needs to be.)
- Choose group members with varied opinions who are willing to express them (your closest friends are not necessarily the best choices).

Time, place, and frequency of meetings:

- Find a regular place and time.
- Decide how frequently you will meet and how long the sessions will be.
- Make your meeting schedule as consistent as possible—that way there is less chance of anyone forgetting a meeting.

Purpose, activities, and group maintenance:

- Establish the overall purpose of your group (for example, to read the class text or to work on a research project your group has been assigned).
- Set an agenda for *each* group session; figure out how you will accomplish each task and how much time you will need.
- Decide how you will accomplish the group tasks of staying focused, getting everyone to participate, and managing your time.
- Form a telephone tree to communicate changes in meeting time, place, or agenda.

Sample format for a session:

1. Check in: People report how they are doing and what they have accomplished with this week's work.
2. If roles have not been previously decided, the group chooses who will facilitate, keep time, and intervene if things get out of hand.
3. Group decides on the order of activities and how much time it will spend on each activity.
4. Group works from one activity to the next.
5. Timekeeper periodically reminds group of time remaining.
6. Group decides tasks for the next meeting.
7. Each member quickly shares her experience of the meeting. Based on this feedback the group makes appropriate adjustments for the next meeting.
8. Facilitator summarizes all agreements made during the group session.
9. Group confirms next meeting's time and place.

Other tips:

- Every group must find its own rhythm, so give your group time.
- As with individuals, groups experience ups and downs.
- One meeting may be terrific; the next may feel much less productive.
- Motivation may vary from member to member and even within the same member.
- If members drop out, those remaining might feel hurt or confused.

One of the important lessons of running a project or study group is staying responsive to each member while not forgetting the purpose and needs of the whole group. The beginning check-in allows the group to pay attention to each member's needs and learning issues, and this information can help the group plan its time.

7.7 • Murphy's Laws of Big and Small Projects

You've heard of Murphy's law, the one that goes "If anything can go wrong, it will?" The law especially applies to managing academic projects.

Minerva's Law

The unexpected is just that: something you don't foresee in your daily plans. The other side of Murphy's Law is Minerva's Law, which holds that preparation can often avert disaster. Learn to practice the art of anticipation, and you might be able to avoid some of the obstacles that life can—and will—throw onto your path.

Here is one way to anticipate the unexpected:

1. Identify a priority: something you need or want to do today, this week, or this semester. Maybe it's a project for school, a job interview, or attending your child's soccer game.

2. Write out this priority as clearly as you can. Or, if you'd prefer, draw or visualize it, or describe it to a friend.

3. Imagine yourself doing the priority. See your surroundings. See the steps you go through.

4. Notice the "usual stuff" that can get in the way:
   Are you distracted, or under a time crunch?
   Do you have all the information or material that you need?
   Do you care enough to follow through?
   Have you scheduled too many things for the same time?

5. Now, try to imagine something happening that normally would not be a part of your plans. Some examples of unexpected obstacles are:
   Public transportation breaks down on the morning of your job interview.
   Your project notes are accidentally thrown away.
   Your child's game is cancelled at the last minute.

6. Create a strategy for dealing with obstacles you can control, such as scheduling your time and gathering the information you need. Also, assume that unanticipated things can happen, and try to plan for those, too. For example, decide you will leave for your job interview a half-hour earlier than you think is necessary.

7. After you have tackled your priority, ask yourself how successful you were in practicing the art of anticipation.

Murphy's Laws of Academic Projects

10.   The less time you have to complete a project, the more things will go wrong.

9.   If there's even a remote chance of running out of something—paper, stamina, ideas, time, brain cells, sanity—you will.

8.   Law 9 particularly applies to vital supplies that you only discover you need at 3am, and morning will be too late.

7.   You are particularly vulnerable to The Worst Case Scenario during the 48-hour period before your project is due. Watch out. Laws 6-3 not only <u>can</u>, but most likely <u>will</u>, happen to you.

6.   Your roommate or significant other contracts a nasty but of course extremely contagious flu.

5.   Your appendix starts to act up. Worse, your cat's appendix starts to act up, and you just <u>can't</u> leave him alone at the vet.

4.   A thief breaks into your study area, and inexplicably steals ONLY your project notes and your sole hard copy.

3.   Your computer chooses this exact moment to crash. Etc.

2.   If you've often been a victim of Murphy's Law, you can continue in your bad luck. There's no upper limit.

1.   If you've had relatively good luck, and haven't yet been the victim of Murphy's Law, your time will soon come.

Avoid Murphy's Laws: plan for the unexpected, since it ALWAYS happens!

● *Activity 7.1*

Think about the projects assigned in your classes this semester. Select one of these projects. List the steps you'll need in order to do this project and estimate how long each step will take.

Name .... Date ....

● *Activity 7.2*

Based on your observations and experience, create three additional Murphy's Laws on completing projects. Describe how each law has affected you or someone you know.

8

Mastering Quizzes, Tests, Midterms, and Finals

For many subjects, the best, and sometimes only, means of assessing if a student has learned the material is through tests. Learning how to prepare for tests, as well as how to do your best in those pressured situations, will help you succeed, even if tests are not your preferred way to show what you know.

The purpose of this chapter is for you to:

- Develop different preparation techniques for multiple-choice, short-answer, and essay tests
- Master test-taking strategies
- Realize how to use the test day to your advantage
- Learn how to handle final exams

8.1 • Preparing for Multiple-Choice and Short-Answer Questions

The trick to preparing for these questions is to be active in the study process. The more senses you use and the more involved you are, the more you'll remember. But, keep in mind, doing well on these tests is not just about memory. It's also about understanding the material.

Some tips:

- Identify important terms, names, dates, definitions from class or the readings. Make a list of all this information. Create flash cards (3" × 5" or larger) of all the important information. Write terms, names, or dates on one side of the card and the definition or explanation on the other. Carry the flash cards with you so you can flip through them at spare moments.

- Use Post-it® notes to write down information you want to remember. Post them everywhere.

- Use as many of your senses as you can to reinforce the material: Talk out loud, move as you talk, beat out a rhythm as you read your notes out loud.

- Put some information on cassette tapes. Listen to them as you walk to class or when you're driving (best not to use this method if you're hitting a lot of traffic or using mountainous, curving roads!).

- Condense all the material into one or two pages. The act of condensing will force you to actively sort through the information and categorize it, which will help you remember it.

- Make big, colorful maps that show the relationships among parts of the material. Or create charts using some of the information. Use large flip chart paper or newsprint if you have it, or tape several 8-1/2 × 11 sheets of paper together.

- Look at past exams to see how the questions are constructed. Make up your own test questions.

- Study with one of your more focused classmates.

- Copy over your notes. As you copy, recite the material, visualize it, draw boxes around the most important information, and put it in your own words.

- Study as if you're taking an essay exam. That way you'll be able to relate bits of material to each other.

- Identify any terms, principles, or definitions that are still unclear to you. Find other books or journal articles with better or clearer information.

- Participate in a study group.

We use both sides of our brain—the intuitive, creative side as well as the logical side—for thinking, and the more you can utilize all of your brain, the better you'll be able to remember facts and information. Two really effective ways are *creating mental pictures* and *mnemonics*.

Suppose you're trying to remember the 1864 Geneva Convention. Picture a room filled with people drinking Geneva Beer, which has the date 1864 on the label. Make your picture as silly, vivid, ridiculous, colorful, or weird as you like.

Suppose you're trying to remember a string of facts or theories for any other collection of data. Use the first letter of each word (or each key word) to create a sentence—the crazier the better. If you want to recall the order of the first eight elements in the periodic table—hydrogen, helium, lithium, beryllium, boron, carbon, nitrogen, oxygen—you could make up this sentence: Hairy Herman Likes Beastly Bozos Carrying Naughty Oxen.

8.2 • Preparing for Essay Questions

Take an active approach: Learn to think like your professor. An effective strategy includes reviewing common essay terms, paying attention to what your professor emphasizes in class, and creating and answering your own essay questions.

Learn the language:

Essay terms tend to mean the same across disciplines.

- *Analyze*: Break the issue apart and discuss each point.
- *Comment/Discuss*: Broad terms that mean talk about the issues in an organized way.
- *Compare and contrast*: Show the similarities and the differences.
- *Define*: Tell what a word or phrase means.
- *Demonstrate*: Support a position with facts, experience, or theories.
- *Describe*: Help the reader understand something by "showing."
- *Evaluate*: Come to conclusions about the worth of something.
- *Explain*: Tell and give reasons.
- *Give examples/Illustrate*: Provide specific instances.
- *Identify*: Name.
- *Justify/Prove*: Use strong reasons to explain your position.
- *List*: Give several named items.
- *Prove*: Provide strong reasons or evidence.
- *Summarize*: See Chapter 5.

Take stock of the course material:

- Look at any tests or quizzes you've taken in this course.
- Ask for sample exams. If you get them, consider them gold. Study the construction of the questions.
- Review your class and text notes. Look for the information your professor considers important.
- Review end-of-chapter questions and summaries.

Take your own essays!

Construct your own essay questions by using the language of essay tests, the format of questions in your class text, and your knowledge of your professor's way of thinking.

- Time yourself and eliminate distractions. Re-create the same conditions you'll have on the test day.
- Read your own questions very carefully. Mark all key words. Consider making a list of each key word or phrase so they don't start to run together.
- Make a plan. Do one question at a time.
- Make a list or map of what you want to talk about.

- If professors give you practice questions, of course take these too. Consider showing your responses to your professor and asking for feedback on ways you could improve.

Evaluate your responses:

- When you're done, put your answers away. (With time you can see your responses more clearly.)
- Look at your stronger and weaker parts. Revise the weaker parts. Enhance the stronger ones if you can.
- Read over your new responses and evaluate again.

Some questions to help you evaluate your own essays:

- Did you answer all parts of every question asked?
- Did you treat some parts more in depth than others? Did you handle some parts more superficially than was appropriate?
- How easy was it to follow the logic and organization of your essay?
- What three things do you want to remember when you're taking the real exam? (Write these down so you won't forget!)

8.3 • Taking Multiple-Choice and Short-Answer Tests

Both multiple-choice and short-answer questions are designed to force you to make very careful distinctions. In multiple choice questions, the answers might be so similar that, if you're not careful, you could misread something.

Tips for all short answer questions (multiple–choice, true/false, fill–in–the–blanks):

- Be careful when reading these words, which are "all or nothing" terms:

never	*nothing*	*only*
every time	*always*	*whenever*
everything	*definitely*	*certain*

- Be careful when reading numbers or years. It's very easy to reverse digits or somehow misread them.

- Be careful when reading words that suggest numbers or quantities:

increased	*couple (usually two)*	*less*
many	*few (two or three)*	*all*
decreased	*several (about five)*	*more*
none	*additional*	

- Be careful when reading words that signal an opposite or some change in thinking:

but	*except*	*nonetheless*
however	*nevertheless*	*on the other hand*

- Be careful when reading words that signal time or sequence:

previous	*already*	*latter*
before	*eventually*	*former*
not until	*introductory*	*initial*
after	*next*	*middle*
later	*final*	*first, fourth, etc.*
subsequent		

Tips for multiple–choice questions:

1. No matter how sure you are that you recognize the best choice, read all the choices before selecting your answer.

2. Be clear about how many choices you can select. Usually, it's one, but make sure.

3. Look at the construction of the question carefully. Some professors use "all of the above" and "none of the above" as choices. For "none of the above" to be true, none of the statements can be correct. In order for "all of the above" to be the correct choice, *every* part of *every* choice must be true.

4. Even if you don't have a clue, guess. With four choices, by guessing you have a 25% chance of getting it right.

5. Try to eliminate at least one choice. Your chances of getting the answer right will increase significantly.

6. You may find that other parts of the test will provide hints for answering multiple-choice questions.

Even though there are only two choices in true/false questions, they do tend to be tricky, so take your time. Matching questions are especially challenging if you're rushing or have any difficulty with spatial relationships. If you misalign one of your answers by mistake, you will miss other questions as well. So go back and double check to make sure your lines are where you intended. For all short-answer and multiple-choice questions, guess but mark those that you're unsure of. Go back to them when you've finished the rest of the exam.

Hey, it's Mr. Question-Person *!*

Each week Mr. Question-Person roams the campus armed with only a notebook and camera, seeking answers to today's hard student questions. He strikes without warning, so watch out: maybe this week you'll find yourself in Mr. Question-Person!

This week's question: **What's your strategy for multiple choice and short answer tests?**

Omar L.
Major:
Linguistics

"I figure out what all the key words are and make sure I understand them. Most seem to be Franco-Germanic origin."

Keshawn A.
Major:
Statistics

"I always answer, even if I'm not sure. And I up the odds by trying to eliminate at least one choice. Want to bet which one?"

Nathan J.
Major:
Computer Science

"Since 'all' or 'none of the above' questions can be tricky, I leave 17% more time for them."

Cherie D.
Major:
Aesthetics

"Like, what's so special about being right? My answers are always artistically relevant."

8.4 • Taking Essay Tests

If you have a choice, selecting the best essay to answer is a critical part of taking an exam or quiz successfully. And no matter what, be sure to read the question(s) carefully.

Before you begin writing:

- Read over all the essay questions and make sure you understand what each is asking you to do.
- Identify all the key words.
- Choose the essay(s) you will answer.
- Develop a strategy: make a list of what you'll cover before you plunge in.
- Feel free to add to the list after you've begun to write.
- Keep returning to the list to make sure you're covering everything.

Organizing your answer:

- Restate the question in the beginning of your answer. You do not need to have a fancy introduction.
- Use the construction of the question to help you organize your essay. For example, if the question asks you to identify three causes for x, then start each section with another cause. Make it very clear when you're identifying a new cause: underline, use bold lettering, or capital letters.
- To show your reader you are moving from one point to another, use words that provide clues, such as *the first, the second, next, furthermore, however, in addition.*
- Keep rereading the question so you don't drift away and end up answering something else.
- Leave enough time to reread your essay
- Make sure you've answered all the parts of each question.
- Make sure you've answered ONLY the question asked.

Other things to remember:

- Don't worry about being elegant, just be clear.
- Avoid arrows or writing in the margins (But, if you've got to, then do it and write an apology on the exam.)
- Get to the point and keep your information organized and specifically related to your essay topic. Students often just dump information into their answers without sorting it out for the professor. Sometimes professors have to "go fishing" for answers, and they don't find what you think is there. Remember, when professors are in the middle of reading exams, it's very easy for them to miss buried treasures.
- Avoid using terms, abbreviations, and language that only you understand. A professor reading your work will not know your mental shorthand!

You probably will come to the test with various facts, formulae, mnemonics, and other information in your head that you've collected while studying. Before even reading the questions, take a few minutes to write this information down. Otherwise, you might either get panicky when you see the questions or get sidetracked by a question and forget some pertinent information. Having this information available will anchor you and maybe help you understand the scope of the questions.

8.5 • On the Day of Your Test

To increase your success, here are some things you can do.

Getting there and settling in:

- A few days before, check out the testing room (if it's a new location). Make sure you know how to get there so you don't waste a moment.

- If you make plans to meet someone after the exam, give yourself plenty of time. (Worrying about being late as you're taking an exam will distract you.)

- Wear comfortable clothes for the room you're in. Layers are generally safe (so you can take off a sweater or sweatshirt, or put one on).

- Arrive early.

- Get the seat you want. If you sit by the door, will you be disturbed by hallway noises? If you sit by a window, will you be distracted by outside noises or views? Will the extra light be helpful? If you need extra room, consider taking an end seat.

- Take out your supplies and set them up. Find a place for your coat (jacket, umbrella) so it won't be in your way or anyone else's.

Begin the test to your advantage:

We highly recommend you read all the directions first. Also read all the essay choices. Be totally clear about what you're expected to do.

- Know how many questions you have to answer and if you have any choices.

- Know how many points you'll get for each question.

- Make a game plan.

- Decide which questions you'll answer if you have a choice.

- Decide what order you'll answer them in (just because something is first, doesn't mean you have to do it first).

- Decide how long you'll spend on each part (usually the more points something is worth, the more time you'll want to spend on that portion).

- Breathe deeply.

- Visualize being successful (coming up with answers, feeling good after the test is over).

- Use positive self-talk. Tell yourself such things as: "I can do it." "I know this." "In five minutes, that information is going to pop into my brain."

- Remind yourself to check your time every 10–15 minutes to make sure you aren't overfocusing on any one section.

- When you come across a question you can't answer, don't panic. Mark it with a big star (or whatever symbol appeals to you) and come back to it later.

- Check to be sure you answered all the questions on the test.

 *If and when you find yourself getting distracted, pull yourself back. Don't get annoyed with yourself: It happens to us all.*

Don't forget the essentials

tissues	paper
eyeglasses	pens and pencils
watch	highlighter
calculator (if a math test and a calculator is allowed)	hard candy or mints

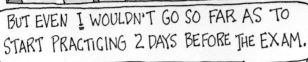

8.6 • Final Exam Fever: The Chills and Thrills

Final exams have a life of their own. The conversation around you is buzzing with concerns about exams. People who didn't study before are now cramming. The circles under students' eyes are around their knees! Everyone knows the end is almost here. For some people, final exam period is exhilarating; for others, it's gruesome.

Consider how finals are different from other tests:

- You now have lots of information on your progress in your courses. This knowledge will help you decide how much time you need to prepare for each exam.

- You have an idea about the kind of test questions your teachers will give.

- Pacing becomes even more important as you go from exam to exam. What you study first, second, and third will partly depend on how much time you have between exams and the order of the exams.

- You might have the feeling of time really speeding up or slowing down. It might seem as if you have entered into an intense world where everyone's main thoughts revolve around exams.

Allocate your study time by determining:

- How much each final is worth of the total course grade. Review the grading section of all your syllabi. You might choose to spend more time preparing for exams that will be a larger percentage of your final grade.

- How well you're already doing in each class.

- How important it is for you to get a good grade. For example, you might choose to study more for a class in your major than for an elective.

- How many credits each course is worth. It may make sense for you to study more for a three-credit than a one- or two-credit course.

- How much material the final exam will cover. Exams that include the entire semester's work will obviously take more study time.

- Whether you're working for a letter grade or pass/fail.

- What type of exam you'll have in each course.

- How much you can or want to push your physical limits. Some people sleep less during this time, figuring they can catch up later. For many people, this is an extremely ineffective strategy.

Treat your own exam fever:

1. Remember that you're not getting graded on how intense or nervous you are, but on how well you show that you know the material. Don't feel you have to whip yourself into a frenzy just because others around you are crazed. If being around exam fever distracts you, limit your contact with those individuals showing symptoms.

2. Don't get strung out on too much caffeine or sugar. It won't help if you are too wound up to sleep.

3. Even if the intensity works for you, still give yourself breaks. They will help you come at the material with a new lens.

4. Get some exercise.

● *Activity 8.1*

Review the material in this chapter. Apply what you've learned to create a ten-item short-answer test on any information from Chapters 2 to 7.

Name .... Date ....

• *Activity 8.2*

Look in the syllabus from one of your classes to find out when your next test or quiz is scheduled. Look at the cartoon in "On the Day of Your Test" and imagine yourself as the main character. Draw or describe what you would do to prepare for a test and what you might forget to do. Write some dialogue about what you might say to Chen or Nathan and what he might say to you.

9

Professors Are People, Too

Some of the most important relationships you'll develop in college are with your professors. On the academic side, you need to learn how your professors organize and present material, what their expectations are, and appropriate ways to negotiate the various issues that can arise in college. On the personal side, you need to understand at least a little about who your professor is and what mutually respectful behavior means.

The purpose of this chapter is for you to:

- Discover what a valuable tool each syllabus is
- Assess your professors' classroom styles as a way of increasing your efficiency as a learner
- Develop techniques for listening to lectures and presentations and for participating in class activities
- Learn how to evaluate and effectively use faculty feedback
- Determine when, how, and why to schedule a conference with your professor
- Increase your confidence in considering if, when, and why you might feel uncomfortable with your professor, and what to do in this situation
- Clarify what it means to cheat or plagiarize and learn how to avoid doing either

9.1 • Loving Your Syllabus

Befriend your syllabus. Get to know it well. Do not throw it away. Do not use it to line the parakeet's cage. Read and re-read your syllabus until you are truly familiar with it. Why? Because the syllabus is an informal contract between you and your professor. Once you receive your syllabus, your professor will hold you to all the information and instructions it contains.

Questions your syllabus should answer:

- What is the grading policy?
- What are the attendance and lateness policies?
- What are the policies for late or missing work?
- What are the due dates for readings, papers, projects, and other assignments?
- How do you locate the professor? What are her office hours and location?
- What are the expectations for class participation?
- Do opportunities exist for extra credit?
- What are the cheating/plagiarism policies?
- What is the complete class schedule, including holidays?

Make it easy on yourself:

- Highlight important dates, such as quizzes and tests, as well as due dates for projects and papers.
- Write these dates in your calendar.
- Review each syllabus every week and feel free to write comments on it.
- Ask the professor questions if anything is unclear: Professors appreciate student interest.
- Understand that from time to time a professor might adjust a syllabus. Write any adjustments in your syllabus, and make changes in your calendar accordingly.
- Make at least one additional copy of each syllabus. Place one copy in your class file or notebook where you can find it easily. Make a separate file of all your syllabi.

 *Believe us, professors can go ballistic when a student claims not to know about a critical assignment or deadline that is right there in the syllabus.*

9.2 • Assessing Your Professor's Classroom Style

Every professor has his own way of organizing and pacing the class, treating the material, giving assignments, and letting you know what he cares about. Once you figure out each professor's style, you can choose how to adjust your behavior to get the most of the class. Here's a checklist to help you describe your professor's teaching style and what you can do to accommodate. Use this checklist for each of your professors.

Assessing Your Professor's Classroom Style

WHAT YOUR PROFESSOR DOES	WHAT YOU CAN DO TO ADAPT
1. How does your professor begin class?	
Asks questions or invites students' questions	Come prepared with questions.
Reviews the last class.	Compare your assessment of last class with his and fill in any gaps in your notes.
Provides an overview of the day's class.	Write down overview verbatim and keep referring to it as you take notes.
Launches into a lecture presentation.	Get there extra early; make sure you're really ready to begin class.
2. How does your professor signal what's important?	
Uses tone of voice (excited? dramatic?) or volume.	Develop a code (for example, a star) for identifying what's important; sit where you can hear your professor's voice.
Uses phrases such as "This is important!" and "This will be on the test!".	Write it down; see above.
Spends a lot of time on one or two topics.	Look for distinct aspects of the material, such as steps, definitions, types.

WHAT YOUR PROFESSOR DOES	WHAT YOU CAN DO TO ADAPT
Puts information on the board or gives handouts.	Copy board verbatim and make sure to take notes of whatever details are given verbally about this information; use handouts if your professor refers to them; otherwise, wait until after class to read them to avoid getting distracted.

3. How does your professor organize the class?

Arranges material topically or chronologically (by time period? by stage?)	Take notes on each topic.
Arranges material randomly.	Be as prepared as possible; take everything down; sort out the information later.
Follows the order of the text.	Take marginal notes right in your text.
Uses students' questions to organize the class.	Write your notes from both the questions and the answers.
Addresses material not specifically covered in the text.	Capture as much as you can in class; sort it out later; relate the material to the ideas or principles in your text.

4. How much and when does your professor expect students to read?

Doesn't expect everyone to have read text before class.	At least preview the text.
Expects thorough reading of the text before each class.	Read and take notes of text before each class.
Assumes students will read only some parts of the text.	Identify which parts professor feels is most important and read and take notes of those at least.
Varies in his expectations.	Keep asking questions to make sure you understand.

5. What is your professor's delivery style?

Lecture.	Be prepared to take notes; re-read and revise them later.
Lecture, discussion, and exercises.	See above. Come to class with questions and fully participate. Make sure you understand the instructions.
Uses mostly exercises; sets up a lab-type atmosphere.	Make sure you understand instructions; keep getting feedback from teacher.

6. How does your professor make assignments?

Uses syllabus or separate handout.	Keep reviewing syllabus and handout.
Uses a combination of the blackboard and verbal instructions.	Watch board for assignments and copy verbatim; write verbal assignments verbatim; clarify what you don't understand; tape record verbal assignments.
Keeps changing assignments.	Keep asking for new assignment changes; try to get changes in hard copy.
Gives lots of advance time for some assignments and little advance time for others.	Plan your other work ahead as much as possible so you can complete assignments from this class with little lead time.

7. How does your professor end the class?

Ends class suddenly.	Be aware of time; be ready with questions.
Takes a few minutes to review the class session.	Use the review as opportunity to see what your professor thinks was the most critical material covered.
Hands out next assignment.	Don't leave class without the next assignment. Get oral instructions, due date, and other information that accompany the assignment.

9.3 • Listening to Faculty Lectures and Presentations

Actually, it's not just listening that you have to do—it's thinking, following the logic (or lack thereof), and generally trying to make sense of the class material being presented. Listening is a lot of hidden work.

Tips for listening and making sense of class material:

- No matter how confused or unprepared you might be, attend class and get there early. Even if you are lost or "zone out" while some of the material is being presented, you'll still have a framework. You'll also get an idea of what your instructor thinks is important.

- Preview your syllabus before each class. Make sure you know what material the session will be covering.

- Prepare for class by doing the assigned reading (and taking notes). As you read, make a list of areas you're not sure about or questions that you'd like to have answered.

- Bring your syllabus to each class.

Give yourself some goals for each class:

- Identify areas you'd like to learn more about. Then create a list of four to six questions you'd like your professor to answer. (If you have more than six goals or questions, prioritize them.)

- If you're very tired or feel ill, choose fewer areas or questions.

Taking notes in class:

- Date each class session. Leave space to add information later.

- Use the professor's overview of the class session, the syllabus, the text, and your knowledge of what will be covered to form the main topics of your notes.

- Wherever you can, put the information into your own words. You'll probably remember it better.

- When you get to terms or other information you're unsure about, leave space. Don't get traumatized. You can always go back later and add what you need.

- Record all questions your professor asks in class. These may show up later as exam questions.

- If and when you find yourself drifting off, remind yourself to focus. Rather than spending more time getting annoyed at yourself, remember that drifting happens to everyone.

- Be as open as possible to the material. Give yourself a chance to think about it. Listen to what your professor (or other classmates) has to say. If you find yourself disagreeing or tuning out, ask yourself why.

After class:

- No matter how terrific your notes are, review them within 24 hours.

- Look for what's missing, misrecorded, or distorted. Correct it.

- On a regular basis (say, once a week), review your notes. Don't bore yourself. Be active: Recite your notes out loud or cover up parts of them and try to recall the information.

Notes taken during class are never complete. You have to do a lot of guesswork as you're listening. It's not until the class is over that you really know what was covered, how each point relates to the others, and what is truly important. By re-doing your notes you not only remind yourself about the main points, but you're forced to analyze the connections among them. You can see, for example, how a certain issue was mentioned in three different places and, therefore, how important it might be or how it is related to what seemed like three entirely different topics. Reviewing your notes after class, and then weekly, will help you remember your notes better and longer. Also, you often will get a different perspective about the importance of specific topics by comparing your notes with those of another student.

9.4 • Participating in Class Discussions and Small Groups

Okay, maybe you're not one of those people who naturally enjoys participating in class discussions or small groups. There are still good reasons to bite the bullet and do it, even if you're uncomfortable. There are also techniques you can learn that make the experience of participating in class discussions and in small groups a bit more satisfying.

Reasons to participate in class discussions:

- Keeps you awake and connected to the material.

- Lets the professor know what you're thinking, which in turn helps her plan better and reach students more effectively.

- Chances are you'll remember the material better because you are more involved.

- Sometimes part of the grade is based on class participation. (Review the syllabus. Even if the instructor doesn't specifically say that participation counts, look at what she says about good intentions, effort, and giving her feedback.)

- Have a heart. When you're on our side of the desk, you'll know just how frustrating it can be if no one asks a question or makes a comment.

- Asking a question or making a comment could start an interesting line of thought. Through your participation, you might also help other students ease into participating.

Analyze how your teachers relate to their students:

- Does the professor expect students to raise their hands or speak out without signaling?

- Does the professor permit students to interrupt her or other students? (If there is lively discussion, and if your professor is casual about interruptions, you may need to do a little interrupting yourself in order to be heard.)

- How accepting of questions, comments, and suggestions does the professor appear to be? Obviously, the more accepting she is, the more chances you can take in raising issues.

- Do students sit in rows or in a circle? In rows, not everyone can be seen all the time. Either choose a seat that allows you to be visible to the instructor, or make sure that you clearly signal when you'd like to make a point (unless your professor doesn't mind interruptions).

For the very fearful/shy student who dreads speaking in public:

- Participate in a study group. That experience will give you an audience in a smaller setting.

- Write what you want to say before you say it.

- If you're reluctant to answer questions, try asking one of your own.

- Rehearse out loud. Rehearse by yourself or converse about the material with a friend.

- Take a public speaking course.

- Break the ice and talk about your discomfort to friends and teachers.

If you're working in a small group:

- Help keep the group focused. Encourage the group to read all directions and to discuss what's expected.

- Ask group members for their input.

- Keep track of time.

Have you ever had the experience of debating whether or not to ask a particular question or raise a point in class? You waffle back and forth; you say to yourself that it probably is a stupid question and you'll just look dumb if you ask it. Then someone else asks your question, which turns out to be the best question of the day. Everyone thinks the other person is brilliant, and you're left kicking yourself. So, speak up.

9.5 • Using Faculty Feedback

You can learn a lot from the comments that professors make about your work. Often, professors will assess your critical thinking and writing skills, your grasp of the information presented in class and your ability to interpret and apply the knowledge you've gained. You can also learn something about each professor's priorities and expectations, which will help you with your next assignment for each class.

How to work with faculty feedback:

- Make a file of returned work from each of your classes.

- For each class, carefully re-read whatever feedback your professor has given you on each of your assignments, tests, and quizzes.

- Try re-writing all faculty comments and notations by putting them in your own words. Don't forget to include the positive remarks.

- Then put the feedback into categories. Some examples might be:
  write more clearly
  give more information
  organize more effectively
  finish one thought before moving on to another
  stick to the question asked
  be more specific
  be less wordy

- Use faculty feedback to help you take your next quiz or exam, write your next paper, or do your next project.

- If you don't understand a comment or want more information on your strengths, don't hesitate to make an appointment with the professor.

- Even if the comments contain less praise than you'd like, stay open to the ideas. Although in theory most professors believe that it's best to point out both your strengths and your weaknesses, when faced with a big pile of papers, they tend to identify more of your weak areas (and sometimes get a little carried away).

We have to admit that two students in the same class who know exactly the same material might get very different grades. Why? Maybe because one writes in a way his professor can understand. Remember, professors are not mind readers. They can only read what they see on paper. Do whatever you can to make it easier for us to understand you. Take any feedback to heart and consider it a gift. You might also look at faculty comments combined from all your classes. Sometimes you'll see patterns across classes.

9.6 • Meeting with Professors Outside Class

Are you one of those students who would rather not talk to professors outside of class? If so, brace yourself, because there are times when you really have to.

Reasons to make an appointment with your professor:

- You're not clear about your choice of a topic for a paper, or you need more information about an assignment.
- You think you should share information about yourself, such as a medical condition or your family situation.
- You want to put your relationship with your professor on a more personal basis. (We are not suggesting a romantic relationship!)
- You need to explain about upcoming absences.

How to make an appointment with your professor:

- Either call during office hours (printed on the syllabus) or immediately after class ask when you can schedule an appointment. Before class many professors are preoccupied, so it's best not to disturb them at that time.
- Explain the reason briefly. If you don't want to be too specific, use codes, such as "to go over the reading" or "to discuss something personal."
- State how much time you think your appointment will take. This helps the professor mentally prepare for your appointment.

How to prepare for a conference and what to do during the conference:

- Bring appropriate materials, such as your syllabus, the readings, or your notes.
- Decide on two or three goals for your conference, then plan what you want to say. Some people bring a list to remind them. Help the professor understand what you'd like her to know or do.
- Dress as you would for class, not any more casually. If you want to be taken seriously, don't show up in a pajama top or slippers, as a few of our students have done!
- When you start the appointment, remind the professor who you are, what class you're in, and the general purpose of your visit.
- Make sure you get your questions answered and your concerns addressed. Professors sometimes slip into the role of lecturer instead of listener.
- At the end of the meeting, summarize your conversation.

To share or not to share

Some students prefer to share personal information about themselves that might explain their class performance, their role in discussions, or their attitudes. To help you decide, consider such factors as the effect your situation or condition is having on your work, your comfort in revealing this information, the level of trust you have with each professor, the topic of the class, the teacher's personality and style, and the size of the class.

Many professors not only need but want to know if you're having a crisis. However, remember that they can only be listeners: Don't expect them to be counselors. If you're not sure whether to share at all or how much to share with a professor, consult someone you know and trust about these matters, such as your advisor, the school counselor, a reliable second year student. Before sharing, ask the professor if it's okay to tell her something personal that you think is affecting your work. Also, request that your conversation be confidential if this is important to you.

9.7 • Dealing with Absences

Class attendance is a priority for most professors, and it should be for you, too. However, sometimes you can't avoid missing class and in those (hopefully rare) cases, attitude is everything. Handle your necessary absences carefully and responsibly, and you should be OK.

Develop an attitude:

- Read your syllabus carefully regarding your professor's policy on absences.

- Weigh the pros and cons of missing class. Save up your absences for critical times (illness, family emergencies). Trust us: These will come.

- Try not to schedule appointments or anything else within your control during class time.

- If you will be missing class, let your professor know in advance, preferably in a face-to-face conversation.

- Present the situation as directly as possible and acknowledge your decision to be out. Be prepared to have your professor disagree with your decision. You might have consequences to face.

- Ask how you can make up the work and/or send in work due.

- Make arrangements with a classmate to review the class; don't expect your professor to re-teach it.

- If you're genuinely ill or facing some other emergency situation, you might not be able to inform your professor prior to class. Be sure to call as soon as you are able or have a friend call.

 **HOT TIP!** *When you next see your professor, never, ever ask, "Did I miss anything important!"*

Some students are so embarrassed or uncomfortable talking to faculty members, especially about missed class or work, that they will avoid these conversations. Do yourself a favor and approach your professor anyway. Professors notice absences and late assignments. Don't take the chance that your professor will interpret an unacknowledged absence as lack of interest in the class. It's better to be jittery for five minutes than to risk offense.

9.8 • No Whining Allowed: Discussing or Protesting Your Grade in Style

You've slaved for weeks (or days or hours) on an assignment. It's the most effort you've ever managed. When the assignment is returned, you're horrified at your grade. You have every right to question your professor. Before you do, however, prepare yourself.

Analyze the situation:

- Realize that professors differ in their grading philosophies and policies. Try to figure out your professor's approach. Even in the same class, a professor might have a different grading system from one assignment, quiz, or test to the next.

- Understand your professor's system for awarding and deducting points. Read your syllabus, the original assignment, your paper (test, project), and the faculty comments on your paper a few times. If you can, determine how many points each part is worth. Some professors are more "generous" about awarding points for "effort" than others.

- Be clear about what's bothering you. Is it the number of points you lost? Is it the tone of the comments that were made? The content of the comments? Do you feel you weren't adequately recognized for what you know or the work you did?

- Analyze your strengths and weaknesses through someone else's eyes:
  Which parts of the assignment were answered incompletely? Which parts were fully answered?
  Which parts, if any, were actually left out?
  Where were the most points lost? Where were the least points lost?
  If you were grading this paper, what advice would you give?

I WORKED SO HARD ON MY ANALYSIS OF THE NEGATIVE SOCIO-ECONOMIC IMPACT OF SMOKING. CAN YOU EXPLAIN WHERE I LOST POINTS?

YOU DID A GREAT JOB ON THAT PART OF THE ASSIGNMENT. BUT I ALSO ASKED YOU TO EXAMINE THE ECONOMIC BENEFITS FOR COMMUNITIES THAT DEPEND ON THE TOBACCO INDUSTRY. I KNOW IT CAN BE HARD TO ANALYZE A POSITION YOU STRONGLY OPPOSE. NEXT TIME BE MORE OBJECTIVE, AND YOU'LL DO FINE.

I DON'T SUPPOSE A SMALL DONATION TO THE TOBACCO GROWERS BENEVOLENT SOCIETY WOULD BE ENOUGH TO UP MY GRADE TO B+?

GOOD TRY BUT NO CIGAR.

Consult with your professor:

- After consulting your syllabus and analyzing the reasons you lost points, make an appointment. Be sure you've had enough time to cool off so that you can listen well and be at your best.

- Come prepared with specific questions that draw the professor into discussion rather than a trial. No matter what, don't end up accusing or offending your professor.

- Sample questions you could ask are:
  "I'm not sure what criteria you used to award points. Could you explain?"
  "I want to improve, so I'd like to understand what you meant when you wrote this comment."
  "I think I answered this question correctly, according to my notes/text. (Bring these to show.) Could you look at this answer and these notes/text and show me what I did incorrectly?"

- Try to listen without interrupting.

- Take notes of the conversation. Feel free to clarify points or ask your professor to repeat points. Every five or ten minutes summarize your understanding of the reasons for your point deductions. It might be easier for you to hear bits of information and keep checking every so often to make sure you understood correctly.

- At the end of the conversation, also take a moment to summarize. That way you'll be sure you have it all.

- Remember, the goal of this appointment is to learn your professor's system for evaluating a particular paper, project, or test. If your professor has been consistent and has realistic criteria, it would be unreasonable to expect her to change your grade only because you're unhappy.

- Getting additional points might be nice, but the best measure of success is learning what you didn't know.

Going Beyond the Conference

If, after your conference, you still feel you deserve a higher grade, you have the option to pursue a grievance. This involves a step-by-step process outlined in your school's grade grievance policy described in a course catalog or student handbook. We encourage you to talk over your decision with a staff member, another faculty member, or your advisor before following the steps in the policy.

Professors grade work, not students

Sometimes students take grades personally. Students may see their grades as evaluations of the amount of work they have done, their intelligence, their ability to fit into college, or their worth as human beings. A grade is not any of these things. A grade is only a reflection of how clearly a student has communicated the information a professor has asked for. It's easy to forget that professors can evaluate only what's in front of them, not what you have in your head (and heart). On the other hand, we do have to admit that occasionally faculty are inconsistent in applying the same criteria to all student papers.

9.9 • If You Feel Uncomfortable with Your Professor

The huge majority of professors are decent people who care about your intellectual development. Nevertheless, professors are only human: We have to admit that we are capable of the same misjudgments, inappropriate behavior, or breaches of ethical conduct that we see in the rest of society.

Every once in a while a professor may do or say something that makes you uncomfortable. For example, a professor's action or comment may seem hurtful, belittling, excluding, or condescending. You might feel one student or one group of students is given special attention, while another student or group is being slighted. In any of these cases, you might feel as if you have little control, are overreacting, and/or should keep your feelings to yourself. You do have other choices.

What you can do when you're uncomfortable:

- For yourself only, identify what you notice. There is no risk to you, and the process might provide you with additional information that either confirms your feelings or suggests your interpretation was incorrect. Either way, you'll have a bit more control than you may now feel. When identifying what you're noticing, it's best to describe what you are seeing or hearing, without jumping to conclusions.

- The situation in question might be very subtle or blatant. Sometimes you'll see only one side or facet. This situation could occur once and not ever again. Or, you might see something that's part of a pattern.

- Below are a few situations that, unfortunately, could happen:

Situation A: A teacher makes negative remarks about a particular group (gay, older, younger, inner city, suburban, women, men) or leaves unchallenged negative remarks made by someone else.

Situation B: During class students from one group (whites, Blacks, Latinos, Native Americans, Italian Americans) are given less air time, are interrupted more, ignored, or minimally acknowledged for their contributions. Other groups are given more air time, are seldom interrupted or ignored, and frequently acknowledged for their contributions.

Situation C: Some people are allowed to do extra credit work, while others aren't.

Ask yourself questions:

1. What exactly (word by word or as close to it as you can get) was said?
2. What led up to the offending remark or action (step by step if you can remember)?
3. What was the context of the remark or action? What specifically had been happening in the class up until the situation occurred?
4. What did the professor do before, during, and after the situation?
5. What did other students do before, during, and after the situation?
6. Which students were involved (either as recipients or initiators)?
7. What specifically happened that led you to believe that someone or a group of students was favored or treated poorly?

Talk to your advisor, another teacher, a counselor, or a mentor to try to understand both what happened and your own reactions to what happened. You might choose to request a conference with the instructor. At this point you should decide whether to go alone or have someone come with you. Be as specific as possible with your professor.

When you feel you need to go further

Once you have identified the situation and established the facts and your own feelings, you might confirm your conclusion that your professor has engaged in extremely inappropriate or unethical behavior. These are very serious charges. If unfounded, they can cause great harm to someone who might be innocent. But, if you're sure, you may feel the situation should be discussed with someone in a position of authority, such as a department chair, dean, or affirmative action officer. After all, you and every other student have the right to a safe, respectful, and supportive environment. Before you go to the meeting, review whatever notes you have.

Sexual harassment

Sexual harassment is actually a form of discrimination and can include sexual advances, inappropriate touching, assault, or rape, as well as inappropriate jokes, intimate words, and leering. The perpetrator either explicitly or subtly conveys that a student's response to the harassment will affect educational decisions, such as grading. If you have any concerns about sexual harassment, find your school's affirmative action officer, who is trained to address these issues.

9.10 • Why Cheating and Plagiarism Are Hazardous to Your Health

You're under a lot of pressure. You not only want good grades, you feel that you need them: to hold onto financial aid, make dean's list, graduate, get into grad school, or compete in the job market. If you're not prepared for a test, if you've waited too long to start a difficult paper, if you're really lost in one of your classes, if you've got the perfect quote but don't have time to find the page where it came from, you might be tempted to cheat or plagiarize. Don't.

What is cheating?
Cheating is academic dishonesty. It includes bringing unauthorized material to an exam, copying someone else's answers, looking at a test ahead of time without permission, or passing in someone else's work as your own.

What is plagiarism?
Many students are unclear about what plagiarism is, or at least all the forms it can take. It's your responsibility to find out not only what it means in your institution, but also how each of your professors interprets plagiarism.

Very generally, plagiarism means that you present someone else's ideas, words, or phrases as your own. Remember, the rules of plagiarism also apply to material you get off the Internet. Just because the material is on the screen in your room doesn't mean it's yours to claim. Treat this material exactly as you would any other.

How to avoid plagiarism:
Once you know what it is, you can avoid plagiarizing. Here are some options you have:

- Take careful notes when you do your research.

- If you don't have time to take notes in your own words when you first read the material, then copy it verbatim and rephrase it later.

- Put quote marks around phrases, sentences, or paragraphs you've copied verbatim. Double check to make sure your quoting is exact.

- For each direct quote you use, summary you make, or ideas that you read about, make sure to provide accurate bibliographic information (such as author, title, page number, date, place, and publisher) so you won't have to waste a lot of time looking for it later.

- For the exact style of citing this bibliographic information, consult a handbook, your professor, the reference librarian, a tutor.

- When you go to the library, bring lots of change with you so you can Xerox long passages. (And, of course, make sure to provide yourself with the correct bibliographic information you'll need.)

Penalties for cheating or plagiarizing:

The penalties are severe. Here are some of them:

- Getting a zero on the assignment or test in question
- Failing a course
- Being expelled for a semester
- Being dismissed from college without graduating

Other compelling reasons not to cheat or plagiarize:

- You prevent yourself from really knowing the material. One of the best ways (and, for many of us, the only way) to really learn something is to work it out for ourselves, practice it, get involved, and own it.
- You destroy your relationship with your faculty and advisor. When professors assign papers or homework, they are trusting you to do your own work. By cheating or plagiarizing, you betray that trust, and you lessen the quality of your relationship.
- Professors may refuse to recommend you for jobs or special awards or be forced to give you only lukewarm recommendations no matter how hard you've worked to recover your reputation.

Sometimes plagiarism falls into a gray area. Students often get confused about the boundary between writing about information they've learned and copying someone else's idea or expression. If you're unsure about how and when to attribute credit to an author, ask your professor. Most colleges have clear guidelines about plagiarism, and your advisor, professor, or tutoring center staff can help you clarify this issue.

● *Activity 9.1*

Look at the cartoon for "Assessing Your Professor's Classroom Style". Recreate this cartoon with you as the caller of 1–800-TEACHER. To help you redo the cartoon, consider these questions:

● Which of your teachers are you checking out?

● What information do you want to find out about that person's teaching style?

● What action do you decide to take as a result of the information you are getting?

● If you decide to put one of your friends in the cartoon, which friend have you selected?

• *Activity 9.2*

Gather together your syllabi from all your classes. Compare them for the following information:

- Grading systems and possibility of extra credit work
- Number and type of assignments
- Policies on absences and lateness

Now describe what you are learning about each of your teachers' expectations. Is there any information not on a syllabus that you would like to know? The next time you see that professor, be sure to ask.

10

Connecting with Yourself and Others

College is a time of transformation. You're gaining knowledge, skills and experience, establishing academic partnerships with professors, and interacting as a peer with fellow students. But it's also a time when personal growth—developing your independence, boundaries, integrity, and compassion—can be the richest achievement of all.

The purpose of this chapter is for you to:

- Determine when and why you might need to take a stand
- Learn ways to say no or not so much
- Develop one method for talking through disagreements
- Explore how to receive criticism and use it to your advantage
- Understand how your family might be affected by your college experience and enhance your communication with them
- Reconsider the inevitable: homesickness or longing for the "good old days"

10.1 • Taking a Stand

Let's say you have a friend who shows up unannounced to study with you for your upcoming exam. You really enjoy being with this person. It would be very tempting to study with him. But every time you get together, you end up socializing and not getting the work done. For times like these, you just have to take a stand. In this case you'd be turning down the companionship of a friend. In other cases you might have to express an unpopular or uncommon opinion, take time for yourself instead of giving it to others, reduce your involvements, or say no. How do you know when to take a stand?

Examples of situations that could prompt you to take a stand:

- Several people in class take one viewpoint. You have another and feel strongly about it.

- You're involved in an exam study group and no one is listening to anyone else.

- Your friend is very late, not unusual for him. You're really tired of waiting.

- Your boss often asks you to work a double shift. Today, he asks you again. You've already finished one shift, and you're drained.

- Your friend asks for a favor that will distract you from the studying you need to do.

What we're really talking about is having faith in yourself and taking responsibility for your own needs. It's not about being selfish or uncaring, even though sometimes doing what you need to do can feel like you're letting other people down. Often, you just have to make a choice, weighing what you need against what other people are asking of you. Remember, too, that sometimes other people will actually benefit from the fact that you can't accommodate them. The boss who makes sudden requests for overtime work, or the friend who asks for favors at inconvenient times, might be disorganized or insensitive to the needs of others. By taking a stand, you might be encouraging these people to find better alternatives. Your boss might realize he has to make a more workable calendar. Your friend might start to understand that his dependency is unhealthy, and he really can manage by himself.

10.2 • No Is Not a Four-Letter Word

Learning to say no or not so much is essential for surviving and thriving in college. There are so many things that can lure you away from your goals and work. As with many other people skills, this one is easier to talk about than to do. That's why you need to practice saying no and find several different ways of saying it, so that when the time comes, you're ready.

A Dozen Ways To Say No

Hedge:

1. "Let me think about it." (*Take your time getting back to this person.*)
2. "Thanks for thinking of me. I'll let you know next week."
3. "Find me three more days, and I'd be willing to work with you."

Explain:

4. Immediately after the request, spend the next five minutes explaining in great detail all the things you have to do. If your friend is still protesting, add another five minutes of explanation.
5. "I care about you (or whatever your friend needs help with), but my assignment this week is critical, and I don't have time for both."
6. "I'm determined to do really well in this course. I'm sorry, but I need all my time to study."

Negotiate:

7. "If you help me word process this paper (or change the baby's diapers for a week), then I'll have time to help you with...."
8. "I could be available for 30 minutes at 7 P.M. (or another very specific and short time period), but that's all I can give."
9. "Of all the parts of this project that you'd like my help on, I can only do this one." (Choose the smallest and easiest part for you.)

Use humor:

10. "You're kidding, right?"
11. "If you had my life for just one day, you wouldn't even think of asking!"

Be concise:

12. "No!!!!!"

HOT TIP! *You might feel flattered that somebody wants or needs your help. This good feeling won't last very long when you're running late or staying up all night to finish your own assignment because you couldn't say no.*

Before committing yourself, count to ten, and ask yourself

- What are my fears if I say no?
- How can I say no without offending this person?
- If I refuse, and my friend is offended, what does this say about our friendship?
- What are the consequences to this relationship if I say no? If I say yes?

- What are the consequences to my work (home life, other relationships) if I say yes?
- What are the consequences to my self-esteem if I say yes?

10.3 • I'm OK: You're Driving Me Crazy

It's natural to have disagreements with others. Are you a person who would rather avoid them? The trouble is, left unspoken, conflicts do tend to get in the way of studying and having satisfying relationships. Here are some things you can do:

When you disagree with a peer (another student or friend):

- Don't hold in your feelings. They'll only build up and become harder to manage. Express them as soon as possible.

- Take some care in creating/finding the best setting and timing.

- Address the issue in a private conversation and not in the middle of a group discussion. Try not to bring the issue up when either party is tired, too upset, or in a hurry.

- Be specific. For example, instead of saying, "You're so inconsiderate," try saying "I felt angry when you left me at the party."

- Avoid lecturing. Try not to use such phrases as "you should," "you never," "you always," or "you need to."

- Consider the possibility that your friend might have another version of the story or feelings that are different from yours.

- Take the time to listen to your friend's side. Listen to what he says as well as what's underneath. Pay attention to his facial expressions and body language.

- Use a problem-solving approach by finding things you can do that will work better. You may want to discuss your options or even make a list.

- You don't always have to find an immediate solution. Sometimes it's helpful just to explore the issues first, rather than try to fix the problem right away.

- Don't expect miracles. This kind of process takes its own time.

Listening tips:

- Even if it's very hard, try not to interrupt the other person.

- Ask questions. Invite your friend to respond with phrases like, "Could you explain…?" "What happened…?"

- Listen to your tone of voice to make sure you're communicating concern rather than aggression.

- Even if you know your friend very well, don't assume what he will say.

- Give yourself and your friend a chance to think about the situation. (Some people need more time to process this kind of information than others.)

- In many situations, eye contact can help bridge misunderstandings.

Conversation starters:

- "Could we discuss what happened at the party? Where and when should we have this conversation?"

- "Something is bothering me, and I'd really like to talk about it soon because I value our friendship. Could we discuss it after dinner?"

Attributing blame is a tricky thing. Sometimes we blame everyone and fail to really look at our own role; sometimes we blame ourselves without looking at who or what else was influencing the situation. In any case, these attitudes can become blocks to communication.

Many researchers who study conflict resolution recommend using "I" messages as a powerful way of acknowledging and accepting responsibility for our feelings. The basic format for "I" messages is: "I felt _____ [furious] when you _____ [didn't include me] because _____ [we always used to do that together and I expected to be included]." It might seem awkward, but try it: This way of phrasing can be a lot easier for the other party to hear.

10.4 • Handling Criticism: Welcome to the Real World

Have you ever gotten negative feedback—about your behavior, skills, knowledge, values, personality, or appearance? If you haven't encountered criticism before, you will in college. Handling criticism—that is, listening to it, sorting out the helpful from the unhelpful, learning from it, and responding to it—is one of the most important skills you'll need in college (and in life).

Don't let the myths of criticism get in your way:

Myth 1: Once you really have mastered something, you don't have to worry about criticism. Only inexperienced and unprofessional people get criticized.

Truth: Feedback that analyzes both the positive and negative aspects of our work is essential to lifelong growth. Faculty frequently critique each other's work, and they evaluate student work as a regular part of their job. No matter how hard we try, no matter how many years of experience we have, we still only have one—our own—perspective. Accurate criticism, as hard as it may be to hear, offers us a chance to widen our lens.

Myth 2: If a friend criticizes you, she's not really a friend.

Truth: It takes courage to tell someone something that's not totally positive. A good friend, one who really cares about you, wants to see you grow and is willing to chance sharing her perceptions.

Myth 3: Making changes because you're criticized is a weakness.

Truth: It takes determination and effort to change. Changes resulting in greater effectiveness show flexibility and personal strength, critical traits for school, work, satisfying friendships, and family life.

Use these strategies for handling criticism:

1. Don't settle for vague or general remarks. Ask questions. ("You said I was immature. Could you give me some examples?")

2. Summarize your understanding of the criticism.

3. Think about the criticism. You do not have to react to it right now. As with disagreements, in many cases the criticism will be clearer or more useful if you take time to think about it.

4. Don't blow the criticism out of proportion. If your friend made ten positive observations and one that seemed negative, don't obsess on the one critical remark and forget about all the compliments.

5. Decide which, if any, feedback you want to use. Sort out the accurate from the inaccurate.

6. Remember that you can disagree with any or all criticism.

7. If you decide a point is true and you wish to address it, make an action plan and keep checking in on your yourself.

8. Sometimes it's appropriate to apologize. For many of us, saying "I'm sorry" is extremely difficult.

Pay attention to how you feel about the criticism. Sometimes feeling uncomfortable is a sign that the criticism is accurate. On the other hand, be sure to evaluate the person making the criticism. Do you generally trust his observations and intentions? Sometimes people will project onto others those patterns they don't like or find hard to acknowledge in themselves.

10.5 • College Is a Family Affair

Believe it or not, your family (whoever you consider as family—parents, significant other, spouse, friends) goes to college with you. Maybe they don't go to classes, take exams, or do papers, but they indirectly experience this new phase in your life. While they want you to flourish, they don't want to be left behind.

When you're feeling the sting of your family's demands, consider these questions:

- Are your family's demands a cry for reassurance from you? Do they need to hear you will still communicate regularly, make plans to spend time together, and, most importantly, continue to care?

- Are their demands an effort to maintain control over you even when it's inappropriate?

- Are their demands an expression of concern for your well-being? Are they nervous about the newness of your environment or the fact that they can't ensure your safety? Could your spouse or friends possibly be a little jealous about this big change in your life?

Suggestions:

- Have regular discussions about what specifically is going well between you, and what you each need.

- If they're worried that you can't handle the new changes and challenges in your life, show them that you're doing well.

- Let them know you still need them and care. And don't forget that you can still ask for advice.

- Above all, be patient with your family and with yourself. These transitions take time. Just because you're now in college, don't expect your family to revise their expectations and behavior automatically.

When You Long for the Good Old Days

The flip side of being excited about college is longing for the life you used to have. When it strikes, this longing (experienced also as homesickness) can feel absolutely terrible. The experience is like grief, and, in a way, you are grieving: You're in the process of changing your old life. We all wish at times we could return to what we already know; it may feel safer or more predictable. It is important to realize that you can have the best of both worlds. Your family is still there, and you're in the process of gaining a whole new you, a developing person with increased skills, knowledge and possibilities.

• Activity 10.1

Think back to a situation in which you wish you had taken a more effective stand. Describe this situation, what steps you took, the result, and what you could have done differently.

• *Activity 10.2*

Review the cartoon in "No is Not a Four-Letter Word". Substitute your own charac-ter for either Amy or Trevor and write new dialogue. Or, if you prefer, describe what advice you might offer them both.

11

You and Your Money

Students today face increasing financial pressure. Tuition continues to rise while financial aid budgets tighten. Many students have to manage jobs while trying to handle a full college load. Learning how to monitor your income and control your expenses can help remove the distraction of fiscal panic from your already demanding life.

The purpose of this chapter is for you to:

- Understand the importance of developing a budget
- Deal more effectively with credit cards
- Develop strategies for stretching limited resources
- Consider some innovative ways to increase your income

11.1 • Budgeting Is an Aerobic Exercise!

Understanding your cash situation is essential whenever you're undergoing financial change and personal transition. Managing your money well will give you more control and less anxiety, which in turn will help you focus more on your studies. (See Budget Worksheet in Appendices.)

When you make a budget, you:

1. List your expenses and income so you produce an itemized account sheet.

2. Actively manage *yourself* so you stick to the budget.

It's relatively easy to make up a budget, but it is an ongoing workout to stay focused and committed to it.

How To Set Up a Simple Budget

Make a list of your estimated monthly expenses, such as:

- Housing (rent/dorm room or mortgage, heat, utilities)
- Telephone (estimated monthly expenses)
- Car (car payments, car insurance, excise tax, gas, tolls, parking, upkeep)
- Food (groceries, eating out, snacks)
- Clothing/uniforms
- Medical (insurance, doctors' bills, prescriptions)
- School (tuition, fees, books and supplies)
- Entertainment (movies, concerts, admissions)
- Incidentals (Xeroxing, postage, transportation, gifts)
- Other (lessons, memberships, public transportation)

Now, also make a list of your available assets:

- Job(s)
- Loan(s)
- Other (savings, gifts, scholarships)

Questions to ask yourself once you have your budget itemized:

- Does my income exceed my expenses? If so, that's terrific!
- If not, what is the deficit each month?
- How much additional money do I need to cover my expenses?
- How and when can I make up this deficit?
- At the end of each month, do I have *any* money left over? Am I just squeaking by?
- If I had an unplanned expense (delayed loan check, late paycheck, extra medical expense), how could I manage?
- Is there a way to reduce my expenses?
- Is there a way to increase my income?

If you are financially interdependent, that is, economically connected to other people (spouse, significant other, parent, children, friend), involve them frequently in your budget review process. They may be able to think of solutions you've missed.

11.2 • The Care and Feeding of Credit Cards

Credit cards are like pets: We grow fond of them. They require a certain amount of management. And, just when we've turned our attention elsewhere, they cause us trouble and cost us money. As with pets, research before "adopting."

Understand the truth about credit card companies:

- Lenders love to target college students.
- They assume those in the 17–22 age group will be naive about reading the "fine print."
- They get credit card holders to accumulate more and more debt by presenting hard-to-refuse offers.

Do credit card comparison shopping:

- Shop around by calling at least three or four credit card companies.
- A credit card company, even one you are already using, might be willing to give you a better deal.
- Be frank: Tell the representative you're looking for the cheapest rate for the longest period of time.
- Do not make any commitments over the telephone. Have the company send an information packet and read it carefully.

Find the interest rate:

- You often have to play detective to find the APR (annual percentage rate of interest) you're being charged. It's frequently in tiny print. Lower APRs mean lower finance charges.
- Many lenders entice prospective cardholders with low introductory interest rates available for three to eleven months, after which time the offer expires and the interest rate can increase dramatically. Unless you are relentless about switching to another credit card, you will eventually be billed at the higher rate.
- Credit card companies do not remind you when your introductory offer runs out. They leave it to you to track and hope you'll forget. Many of us do. If you don't have the patience and the time to keep switching, find one reasonable permanent rate you can live with and stay with that one.

Learn this additional information:

- Your credit limit
- Annual fee, if any
- Fees for late payment and over-the-credit-limit

Take care of your credit cards and use moderation:

- Keep a list of all cards, card numbers, and expiration dates. Never leave cards lying around and report missing cards immediately.
- Think about how many credit cards you need. Unless you have a strong reason, consider using *only one*. You'll have less to monitor and be less tempted to spend.

- Don't even think about trying to avoid paying your bills or paying them late. Late payments can stay on your credit rating for years.

No matter how low the interest, in the long run using credit cards is much more expensive than paying in cash, unless you pay your monthly balance. (Some people use "debit cards" which deduct money from their checking accounts.)

Look for the best methods to manage your debt load: Pay the maximum you can afford on each and every payment. Try to repackage or consolidate your debts. Keep focused on your financial situation and talk to others about methods for staying on top of credit card bills.

11.3 • Stretching Your Limited Resources

Despite your best efforts, if you're a college student, you're probably broke. However, there are ways to stretch your resources to accumulate material items, get services, and have fun without spending much money.

Some Things To Try

Bartering:

- Decide what services or products you can offer. Decide what you need and who could supply it. Decide what is a fair trade and make clear arrangements.

Swapping:

- Have some friends each contribute a few items (clothing, CDs, books, kids' games, or toys). Pile them up and plunge in. Each person chooses items until the selection is depleted. Chances are, you'll end up with something interesting and useful.

Creative present giving:

- Make presents. Give certificates of achievement in beautiful wrapping or fantasy trips to special places.

- Buy inexpensive gifts. The trick is to come up with an interesting explanation about how the gift is relevant to your friend: For example, if you're giving tea bags, in a card you might write, "To help you relax before your next mid-term."

- Give of your time. You could type a friend's paper, cook him a special dinner, or offer babysitting time.

Reallocating and planning ahead:

- See if you can spend less on some items so that you could use the money to buy something else.

- Look for sales.

- Buy essentials before you run out of them and purchase presents early. That way you'll have time to select items that are reasonably priced.

Checking out the freebies:

- Many cities and university towns offer events that are both fun and free. Read the local newspaper or posters for announcements of street fairs, concerts in the park or in churches, lectures, art gallery openings, exhibitions, and movie screenings.

Repulsing impulse buying

We know you may be just dying to have that CD or software, but do you really need it? Most of us buy things on impulse that we don't need or even *really* want. One way to cut down on your impulse buying is to rank on a scale of one to ten (ten being the highest) how critical a particular item or service is to you. Ask yourself what the consequences would be if you didn't have the item or service. If you're really broke, you might want to invest in only those things that rank nine or higher. And, if you can't think of a really good reason, don't even buy that item. Another way to reduce impulse buying is to delay the decision to buy for just one day. Chances are, the purchase won't seem so crucial the next morning.

11.4 • Strategies for Increasing Your Income

Suppose you don't have time for another "real" job, and you're sick of the money running out before the month does. If you've got some spare hours scattered through your schedule, consider a little student-style entrepreneurship.

A few ideas:

- With a couple of friends, set up a small housecleaning service for faculty and staff.
- Offer a pet-walking/feeding/sitting service for college employees who are away on brief trips.
- Be a designated driver for hire.
- Become a paid housesitter (this usually means that you do light housecleaning).
- Join a catering company as an occasional waitperson.
- If you are an artist, do drawings of houses for the homeowners to use as Christmas cards or stationery.
- If you are a film buff, make videos of weddings, anniversaries, religious ceremonies.
- Become a word-processor for hire.
- Fix equipment, bicycles.
- If you are a musician, teach an instrument or play at an event.

11.5 • How To Find $10 When You're Absolutely Broke

Everybody knows college students never, ever have enough money for those unexpected things that crop up. But college students are also quite resourceful and that includes finding small treasures (like coins and dollar bills) in out-of-the-way and not-so-out-of-the-way places.

Go Fishing. Check:

- Pockets (look especially in last season's clothing)
- The bottom of your backpack or purse and all their compartments
- Desk drawers, small dishes, cans, containers, or jars that might be collecting coins
- In between the pages of your books
- Under your bed (especially if you don't clean much), and in couches (yours or others)

Another way to "find" money is to watch what you spend for "incidentals:" snacks, paper, toothpaste. Even though it seems like you aren't spending much at any one time, if you really look you might find that it adds up to a lot more than you think.

To find out what you're really spending, try keeping a log of your daily expenses for two or three months. We know it's not simple, but it's one of the best ways of finding out how you manage money day-to-day.

One of our colleagues kept running out of money each month. Once she started keeping a log, she realized what was happening. Her incidental expenses were almost double what she had budgeted, which amounted to several hundred dollars a month. Once she began keeping within her budget, she quickly saved enough money for a nice holiday.

Name .... Date ....

● *Activity 11.1*

Using the information in "Budgeting Is an Aerobic Exercise," make a monthly budget.
After you've carefully reviewed your budget, what do you notice? Is there anything
you need to do? If so, what?

• *Activity 11.2*

Identify (or even exaggerate) one of your strengths. It can be in any arena: academic, social, spiritual, artistic, or physical. Figure out how this strength could help you augment your income. (Be as fanciful as you'd like.) Look at the cartoon in "Strategies for Increasing Your Income" and make a sign advertising your own service.

·12·

When the Hard Times Come

College life is just that: *life*, with all its ups and downs, joys and challenges. A certain amount of stress is part of even positive situations. You'll see a big difference in the quality of your days if you learn the following: when you're stressed, how well you deal with the causes and effects of stress, what to do in situations that are truly overwhelming, and how to find hope when everything feels pointless.

The purpose of this chapter is for you to:

- Identify your stresses
- Explore styles and strategies for coping with stress
- Learn how to minimize the impact of illness and other times you feel lousy
- Develop ways to cope and continue after the break-up of a romantic relationship
- Deal more effectively with the times you've blown it, especially the really big mistakes
- Take the time to confront whatever may be enticing you away from your academic goals
- Discover the power of persistence

12.1 • Are You Stressed?

Your professor has just announced a surprise project, due next week. Or, you find out your financial aid didn't come through. Welcome to college! No matter how much you try to avoid it, at some point you will feel stressed. Think of stress as those hard-to-deal with emotions and physical sensations you experience when something changes or gets in the way of your routines and goals.

Many people think the causes of stress are external, for example, sudden demands by others. But stress can also be caused by your own desires and needs, such as a driving force to do or avoid something.

Each of us has different causes of stress and different responses to it. What makes you anxious one semester may not seem so trying the next. What stresses you may not bother a friend of yours or affect him in the same way.

Possible Stressful Situations (Figure out your own scale.)

Moderate:

- Checkbook shows you will have a small negative balance until next week
- Argument with a friend or relative
- Bookstore has run out of the required text you haven't bought yet
- More responsibility at work
- First date with someone you might really like
- Not enough time to complete an assignment
- Your child has strep throat
- Negative feedback on an assignment
- Low grade on an exam

Bigger:

- Flunking a class
- Break-up of a significant relationship
- Changing majors
- Getting married
- Not getting along with your roommate
- Losing your job
- Divorce of your parents
- Serious illness of yourself
- Serious illness or death of a close friend, sibling, parent

HOT TIP!

Sometimes the only forces that get us to change in positive ways are things that stress us. The argument you had with your friend may have gotten you to think about yourself in useful ways. The low grade on that quiz may have prompted you to realize that you're overinvolved in community activities and not spending enough time studying.

Make a list of what has caused you stress in the last week, month, and year. The more stresses you've felt, the more important it is for you to be aware that you are vulnerable to not being at your best. Some people even become ill.

Look at your list and ask if there are any ways to eliminate or reduce the causes of unwanted stress. For example, you probably won't be able to eliminate an extremely time-consuming term paper, but you could choose a topic that excites you so the time spent seems very worthwhile.

Keep in mind that many of the stresses listed are truly traumatic, while some are just annoying or even mean something good is happening. Some stress can feel awful or uncomfortable at the time, but may result in something positive.

12.2 • How Do You React to Stress?

There are many ways of responding to stress. See if you identify with any of the styles below or recognize the style of someone you know.

Stress-ee	Response	What It Is	Pros	Cons
	"What a disaster. This is the biggest black hole yet!"	**Catastrophizing** Situation is blown out of proportion	Energizes you to act.	When method is constantly used, it can be tiring on both you and your friends.
	"I'm getting dizzy just thinking about it!"	**Somaticizing** Stress expressed through physical reaction	Let's you know when you're stressed, which can be a clue to take action.	You're in discomfort and distracted from the situation.
	"No big deal, I can handle this."	**Minimizing** Under-rating the seriousness of a situation	Can keep you from panicking and freezing up.	You might miss some of the parts of the problem and not act appropriately. It can prevent you from getting the support you need.
	"When the going gets tough, the tough start planning."	**Action-Oriented** Stress leads to plan of action which is then carried out	Lets you attack the problem, and not wallow in self-pity.	If not well thought out, the plan may not respond to the entire problem.
	"That part of the paper will take 3.45 hours to complete."	**Over-Focusing on the Small Stuff** Concentrating on some details at the expense of others	Allows you to begin to act on the part you're emphasizing.	You'll miss other parts of the problem.
	"Problem? What problem?"	**Ignoring the Problem** Not paying any attention to the stressful situation	If you have a lot of other stresses to deal with and this situation is not a high priority to resolve, sometimes it does make sense to ignore it for awhile.	No solution is possible because no problem is recognized. While you are ignoring the problem, it could get worse.

Getting to know your own style helps you manage stress more effectively

If you're a catastrophizer:
You've got the ability to act, to turn something around. That's great. But, before you jump to conclusions, ask yourself: Am I being realistic? Is this such a big problem? Is there any other way to look at this turn of events? Is this a problem or an opportunity?

If you're a somaticizer:
That stomach ache, headache; those sweaty palms—those physical symptoms may be calling out to you. And, even if you're sure you're not really sick, it still may be a good idea to check them out. At the same time, don't let these symptoms overwhelm you or prevent you from taking action. Find a way to work through these symptoms without running away from the problem.

If you're a minimizer:
It may seem natural to tell yourself that if you just sleep a little less, you'll be able to finish your assignment; or if you don't have enough money for food for the next two days, it won't really matter. Minimizing may help you get through a difficult situation, but it may also compromise your health or the quality of your work. So, when something comes up, like that paper you forgot, try to take a good look at the whole picture.

If you're action–oriented:
If you're over-focusing on the small stuff:
Let's say you have a research paper. You panic. All you can think about is you need five sources, 10 pages, and no spelling mistakes. You're concentrating so hard on these details that you don't take enough time to find a topic you really care about, one that makes the whole assignment worthwhile. So, take a deep breath, and look at the whole assignment.

If you're ignoring the problem:
Suppose you're falling further and further behind in one of your courses, but you're so busy with the others that you put off seeing your professor. Now it's mid-semester and you're scared you'll flunk the course. You think to yourself, "there has to be a better way."

12.3 • Other Stress Strategies

The way you deal with stress is a choice. You don't have to be stuck with one or two ways of responding to stress. In fact, we encourage you to try different approaches. Read the options below. Use as many as you need, adjust them, and/or create your own.

Plan and implement:

- Write a list of what you can do immediately about a stressful situation and what you can do in the long run.
- From your list, prioritize. Then for each of your priority items, make a plan of attack.
- Tackle each item according to your plan.
- Evaluate your approach and change as necessary.

Get support and information:

- Find out how others have dealt with the kind of stress you're facing.
- Get support from friends. Let them know you're going through hard times.

Restore your mental balance:

- Freewrite about how you feel and what the stresses are.
- Write a scene in which you are talking to the things that stress you.
- Write a letter to your spouse or significant other about everything that's been going on. (You don't need to send it.)
- Take a few minutes for yourself (hot bath or shower, read something for fun) before you plunge in and try to act on the situation.
- If you're feeling particularly off-center, do an everyday chore: fold laundry, clean the sink, sweep the floor.
- Get some air, work out, swim, play basketball, dance, meditate, or exercise.
- Pay attention to what your body is telling you. If you have a stomach ache from stress, recognize it and don't push yourself quite as much.
- Even when you're feeling like there's nothing you can do right, find something that is working.
- Try to identify one small joyful or positive thing in your life. Focus on it for a moment, nourish it, draw it.
- Talk to your dog (or someone else's), stroke a cat, follow the path of a fish.
- Change your scenery—go to a new location.
- Punch pillows.
- Get in your car, roll up the windows, and scream as loud as you can.
- Make faces at yourself in the mirror.

12.4 • When You Feel Lousy

Here's the scoop. Contrary to what your body, mind, or heart is telling you, life doesn't stop when you feel lousy. Maybe you're ill; you just got into a big argument with someone you care about; you damaged your car in an accident; or your pet needs surgery. The fact is that you still have college responsibilities—that paper, tomorrow's quiz, a reading assignment, a class presentation, your part of a group project. You may also have to deal with your other regular obligations of a job, internship, and/or family.

We know how tempting it is to cancel the entire day, go back to bed, and pull up the covers. But, before you do, think about the consequences. We've seen too many students lose their credibility with professors and make their situation even worse by thinking a day off was the solution. Many times, it's not. Whichever decisions you make, be sure to consult each class syllabus for its policy on missed classes and work.

Here are some questions to ask yourself:

- Do you have to put absolutely everything aside to take care of yourself or your situation?

- Are you really so sick that you just can't get out of bed for an entire day?

- Are there some college-related responsibilities that you could do even if they take longer than usual and won't come off quite as well?

When you decide to slow down, but still get some college work done:

- Look at your schedule for the day (or whatever time period you'll need to have a modified schedule).

- Prioritize your college-related and other responsibilities. Pick the most important tasks to be done.

- Look at how much time you'll realistically need. Give yourself extra time.

- Make a plan for dealing with each responsibility you're opting out of. (For example, for missed classes in which you will be working on a group project, you'll need to call both your professor and at least one member of your group.)

Before you opt out of taking quizzes or exams, or handing in a paper on time

Unless you're totally incapacitated or have a true emergency such as a hospitalization, death in the family, or car accident that has left you very shaken, think long and hard before bailing out. Professors really don't like it. Sometimes they refuse to give make-up tests. Also, professors might believe that extending deadlines gives one student an unfair advantage over others, a situation they must try to avoid.

12.5 • Dealing with the Breakup of a Relationship

A broken heart can be one of life's most painful experiences. When a relationship that you've cared about and counted on ends—especially when the break-up is not your choice—it can feel like a bomb going off in your life. How in the world are you supposed to manage the other important things, like school, maintaining your other relationships with family and friends, and simply keeping yourself going? It's not easy, but it can be done.

Some things to do or watch out for:

- Everyone will tell you this, but it still is true: Time will make a huge difference in how you feel.

- Pay extra attention to your physical health and appearance. It's easy to over- or undereat, to drink too much, to forget about personal grooming (as in "washing my hair is too much trouble").

- In particular, keep to either your normal exercise routine, or start one, such as making yourself walk every day. Aerobic exercise releases endorphins into your blood, which will make you feel better. We also caution: If you find that you're constantly exercising, realize that you're getting out of balance, and make some changes.

- Don't pretend to feel okay when you don't, but be aware of how much you might be dumping on your friends. Don't overload them. If they tell you that you're beginning to obsess, listen to them, and take it seriously.

- Consider counseling to get you through this hard time. Check out your school's counseling center.

- You may be throwing yourself into your academic work, or you may be avoiding it like the plague. Remember, try for balance. If you're avoiding your academic work, realize that it may be one of the few things right now that you can control. Blowing a semester's good standing is not going to change your situation: It's only going to hurt you more.

- Concentrate on your healing process. You may blame yourself. You may blame your ex. But at some point you will have to let it go. (We know this is easier said than done!) The sooner you can truly move beyond those raw, hurt, angry feelings, the sooner you will be ready for the next phase in your life.

- Once you are feeling a little better, ask yourself if there are any lessons in this situation for you to learn. Is there anything for which you need to take responsibility? Anything that in retrospect you would do differently?

College environments can be like small villages: You might not be able to avoid your ex. Your former significant other might be in one of your classes or live close by. Worst of all, this person might now be involved with one of your friends! Try this visualization: Think about how you'd like to present yourself when you next run into your ex. Whatever inner resources you think you'll need to get through this moment, imagine that you have them within your control. If you think you need to express yourself, visualize how you would do so. Now imagine running into your ex and responding to your own satisfaction.

12.6 • Negotiating Your Way out of the Hot Seat

When you're really stretched for time, you may find yourself unable to keep appointments and commitments.

When you've got to cancel out:

- Choose the right timing, if possible.

- If the timing can't be perfect, set the best stage you can.

- Explain your feelings and the facts. Take responsibility for anything you could have done differently:

    Preferred: "I'm sorry I waited until the last minute."

    Less effective: "Better late than just not showing up."

    You're kidding, right?: "Hey, what's your problem? I'm here now."

- Speak genuinely. Don't be afraid to sound a bit frantic if that's how you feel.

- Don't expect someone to be automatically understanding and accepting.

- Reschedule, immediately if possible. Set a clear time for the new commitment.

- If you're too stressed even to think about other dates, say when you will reschedule and stick to your promise. Most people will give you some slack if you explain the tough circumstances you're in and make new plans that you keep. But, you can't keep disappointing them.

If you keep overextending yourself—for example, because of your desire to keep others happy—take a few minutes to realistically evaluate your schedule and commitments. Start making dates you can keep: Don't plan an evening out if you only have time for coffee. Your crazy schedule won't last forever, and you can make more ambitious plans when things ease up.

12.7 • When You've Really Screwed Up

At the beginning of college, you can probably expect to make at least one big mistake. (For example, you forgot to do an assignment or did the wrong assignment, didn't study for a quiz or exam, or didn't prepare sufficiently for your oral presentation.) If and when you make a big mistake, remember to forgive yourself and learn from the experience.

What to do when you've really blown it:

- Remind yourself these glitches happen to almost every college student starting out.

- Get distance from the situation. Do something active for at least 30 minutes: garden, walk, swim, play an instrument, go shopping.

- Find someone you can talk to (a favorite teacher, advisor, good friend, significant other).

- Try to figure out why the situation happened.

- Try to rectify the situation if at all possible.

For the future

Remember, the most important thing you can do is learn from this experience and use this information to do better next time. Write down what you've learned. It may seem like it's burned into your brain now, but you'd be surprised what you can forget!

Knowing what you now know, look at your schedule for the rest of the semester. Make sure you're clear about what's due and when. Make sure you have the time you need for studying and completing assignments. If you've flunked an assignment or test, set up a conference with your professor and demonstrate your willingness to improve your situation. Reschedule appointments and other commitments if necessary.

12.8 • When You Feel Like You're Losing Control

College can be a great adventure, a time of tremendous growth, discovering independence or a new kind of independence. College also can be a time of experimentation and meeting people with unfamiliar values and styles. The pressure to fit in can be overwhelming.

Some of the many temptations you may encounter:

- To continue smoking even though you'd like to quit or to start smoking
- To overeat, eat too much junk food, starve or purge yourself
- To become sedentary or to overexercize
- To drink more than you should
- To spend money impulsively or to buy things that you cannot afford
- To experiment with drugs in a way that feels detrimental to your health and goals
- To spend more time than you really enjoy with friends whose primary interest seems to be getting high
- To have unprotected sexual contact or any intimate contact that makes you feel uncomfortable

Questions to ask yourself:

- What, if anything, is getting in the way of my academic goals and personal dreams?
- Do I like who I am and who I'm becoming?
- Do I like the people I hang out with?
- Do I feel it's okay if not absolutely everybody likes me or everything I do?
- On a scale of one—100 (100 as the highest), how well am I handling my life now?
- If I'm not happy about how my life is going, can I make necessary changes myself, or do I need assistance?

The thing about control:

The flip side of feeling out of control is feeling you have to be "perfect." Measuring your goals and your self-esteem (your body, relationships, behavior, accomplishments) by the yardstick of perfectionism is really a way of trying to be in total control of your life. Nobody can predict the future with certainty or make everything come out exactly according to plan. A more realistic, and ultimately more satisfying, solution is to think in terms of managing, rather than controlling, what challenges you.

Read the following chart. In the left column are six unrealistic goals about "perfect control." Next to each is an example of a revised goal that allows for each individual to flourish.

PERFECT CONTROL	REVISED GOAL
I have to be right the first time.	If I put in the effort, I can do good work.
I can make everything perfect.	I can manage the important things.
I have to do whatever it takes to fit in.	I am my own person and make my own choices.
To be attractive, I have to have a body like a model.	I know that who I am is more than my body.
I have to have what other people have.	My value as a person is not determined by my possessions.
I have to get the highest grade in class.	I will do my personal best.

When you can't or don't want to do it alone

There are times when you might need help in making a necessary change. Here are some resources to consider: Counseling center; Campus support groups; Alcoholics Anonymous; Narcotics Anonymous; Pastoral counselor; Resident assistant; Any trusted friend or advisor.

12.9 • Before You Give Up

What might now seem so awful or outrageous usually has a way of working out if you just hang in there.

Here are some questions to ask yourself when things look grim:

- Is there one action I could take right now to make even a small difference in this situation?

- Is there someone I can talk to?

- Is there something nonharmful I can do (exercise, a good meal, a small present for myself) to make myself feel temporarily a little better?

 *We are amazed at how even a few days can make such an enormous difference in students' moods and perspectives. In our experience, persisting, even when it feels hopeless, is the single most important action you can take.*

The power of persistence

When you persevere, you are sending very strong messages to yourself. Your willingness to keep focused on what you want to accomplish, your determination to keep going, and your refusal to give up easily all reinforce the idea that you can choose to be a survivor or a winner instead of a victim. Even if you don't fully succeed, you probably will feel much better about yourself if you try.

To energize and inspire yourself to persevere, get to know people who have achieved success against the odds. When you're with a new (or not so new) friend or classmate, listen for opportunities to find out how he achieved a difficult goal. Some questions you might ask are:

- What made the goal difficult?

- What steps did you take?

- As you look back, would you do anything differently?

- How has this achievement helped you?

Remember, it's also important to know when to keep pursuing a goal, and when to stop. Sometimes, if you're really just hitting your head against the wall or if your goal is costing too much of yourself, it can be best to let go and refocus your energies on something new.

September
Dear Angela:

My life is a mess! I couldn't get into the classes I wanted. My best friend and I are fighting over a guy, and now we're hardly speaking. My roommate and I aren't speaking either. And worst of all, I just flunked a quiz. Should I drop out?

Desperately, Dazed

October
Dear Angela:

Well, even though I haven't heard from you, I've decided to fill you in. I'm still in college. Two of my classes are actually turning out OK. That guy I mentioned? Well, I must have been crazy to want him. My best friend and I are tighter than ever, and I made peace with my roommate. But I flunked another Econ test. Do you have any advice?

Eagerly, Semi-Dazed

November
Dear Angela:

Since my last letter, I got up the nerve to make an appointment with my Econ professor. We went over the quizzes and it turns out they're worth only 10 points of the whole grade. I guess I can live with that. All in all, things are going pretty good. Maybe college is turning out OK after all. Thanks for listening.

Gratefully, Un-Dazed

I KNEW SHE'D FIGURE IT OUT.

• *Activity 12.1*

Identify any stresses you've experienced in the last week. (If there are too many, limit yourself to the last day or two.) Step back, and in two or more paragraphs write about any actions you could take that would reduce the stress.

● *Activity 12.2*

Think of a situation when you were in the hot seat with another person: a friend, a romantic partner, or anyone else. Revise the cartoon in "Negotiating Your Way out of the Hot Seat" by including yourself as the main character. Add frames or dialogue if you need them.

• *13* •

(Nearly) Ready for Prime Time

Sometimes we get so involved in hurdling roadblocks that we forget to rejoice in the distance we've traveled and all the experience and knowledge we've gained along the way. Maybe the destination is not yet in sight, but take a moment anyway to celebrate your accomplishments and extend what you've learned.

The purpose of this chapter is for you to:

- Develop strategies to acknowledge and reward your progress and success
- Create ways to show the world what you've achieved
- Realize the advantages of working with a mentor or coach
- Learn when and how to quiet the critical voices in your head, and when to listen
- Refine the art of becoming a star in your own comedy and discover the healing power of laughter
- Find opportunities to apply what you've learned in *Frame by Frame*

13.1 • Reinventing Yourself as a Portable Student

As you've already discovered, entering college means being prepared for almost any contingency.

Here are some other ways to get ready for the unexpected

Have back up plans:

- Substitute childcare arrangements when your child is ill or you can't pick him up at the usual time

- Other ways to get to school/work/internship when your car or public transportation won't cooperate

- Handy explanations when peers or family want more than you can offer

Maintain your ability to act, so you can take advantage of sudden opportunities or turn the negative into the positive:

- Know your goals. If your goal is to be successful in a course, and you just found that you have a paper due in two days, you may choose to adjust your schedule for a day (or a week).

- Calculate the consequence: In order to do the paper and change your schedule in the example above, you may want to ask yourself what tasks or assignments won't get done or done as well.

- Decide if you're willing to take the risk to act (or not to act).

- Once you decide to act, take responsibility for your responses even if the situation doesn't work out completely. Don't blame your decision on anybody else. Don't whine, don't throw a tantrum, and don't obsess. You'll only waste time you probably don't have.

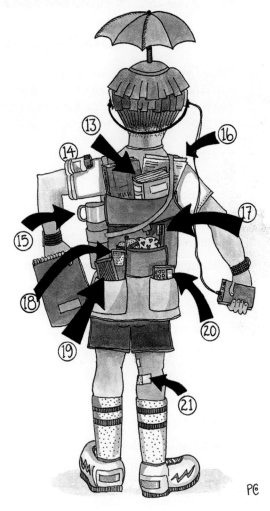

1. Foul weather gear
2. Clip-on sunglasses
3. Beeper for Chinese food that's being delivered
4. Emergency food
5. Stopwatch
6. Pencils, pens, highlighter & ruler
7. Stapler & paperclips
8. Calculator watch with alarm
9. Notebook
10. Shorts for exercise opportunities that might arise unexpectedly
11. Tape recorder for listening to relevant information, and recording notes & ideas
12. Running shoes

13. Required reading
14. Vitamin pills
15. Thermos with hot coffee
16. Class schedules
17. Spare socks, underwear & toothbrush
18. Wallet with library card, public transportation pass, driver's license, phone card, & photo of Gilbert, the family dog
19. Cell phone with memory:
    #1. Mom & Dad
    #2. Roommate
    #3. Dean of Students
    #4. Pizza delivery
20. Electronic organizer & backup day book
21. Spare Band-Aid.

13.2 • Counting Your (Even Small) Successes

Not all your successes are obvious, monumental, or gradable (at least by a professor). The smaller achievements, the ones that often go unnoticed, also show us how much we've grown. Taking the time to acknowledge some of these less obvious accomplishments will keep you motivated and help you stay on track.

Examples of overlooked achievements and successes:

- Deciding to keep an open mind about a professor some students don't like and realizing that you can evaluate for yourself
- Finding a way to spend time with your child *and* do your homework
- Figuring out a new way to take notes
- Revising your piece *again* and seeing how effective it now becomes
- Taking the risk of telling someone in your writing group that her piece was confusing to you
- Locating the articles you need for your term paper
- Finding the courage to ask a question in class
- Reworking your schedule to accommodate a new assignment
- Turning off a distracting TV program
- Learning how to use the library's electronic search procedure
- Making an academic appointment that you've been putting off
- Finding two spelling errors and fixing them before handing in your paper
- Figuring out why you lost those points on the quiz
- Avoiding the temptation to choose a project topic simply because you have material on it
- Recognizing you have too much to do and then saying no when someone asks you to work on a campus event
- Surviving mid-terms
- Listening without interrupting to a friend who's angry with you
- Getting up and out to an early class when you really feel like staying in bed

If you have trouble identifying your small successes, buddy up with a friend and help each other. You can identify small successes either for each project or task you're tackling or for a specific time period, such as a day, week, or month. The success can be microscopic, something you'd never think about if you weren't doing this exercise.

13.3 • Giving Yourself Rewards

Why not reward yourself for your accomplishments? Rewards help emphasize the positive, break the routine, and keep you focused. Choose rewards that are reasonable. You probably don't need a trip around the world on the Concorde to congratulate yourself for completing that report (not that it wouldn't be nice). In addition to material things, also consider nonmaterial things that still give you satisfaction.

Some small (and not so small) ways to reward yourself:

- Take a walk.
- Buy a CD (buy two).
- Get a sitter for the kids and take a break.
- Take a bubble bath.
- Fly a kite.
- Call up an old friend.
- Read the comics.
- Rent a funny movie.
- Work on a jigsaw puzzle.
- Buy a loud tie.
- Shoot some hoops.
- Go on a boat ride.
- Rollerblade.
- Join a health club.
- Take yourself on a picnic.
- Buy yourself some flowers.
- Go to a baseball game.
- Watch a soap opera.
- Forget your diet just this once.
- Have a snack with a friend.
- Listen to live music.
- Spend $5 too much on something frivolous.
- Learn a new dance.
- Color your hair.
- Tinker with your favorite tool.
- Play an instrument.
- Play with your kids' toys (or someone else's) when they're not looking.
- Plan a trip for spring break.

13.4 • Mining for Mentors

One of the best success strategies is finding a mentor, someone who takes a special interest in you and encourages your personal best. A mentor might be a professor; advisor; athletic coach; counselor; second or third year student; someone you trust; someone working in your career field; someone who will take the time for you and respect you. Having a mentor who knows the way things work at your school can also save you enormous time and frustration.

A mentor can:

- Provide information
- Help you look at new aspects
- Help you believe in yourself
- Give honest feedback
- Discuss the hard stuff and kick you in the butt
- Listen and support you in times of crisis
- Help you evaluate what you need to do to solve a problem
- Take pride in your accomplishments, even when they exceed hers
- Respect you and be willing to learn from you
- Let you be yourself when you're with her
- Be interested in what's best for you, without any other agenda

What a mentor doesn't have to, can't, or shouldn't be:

- Perfect
- Entertaining
- Of your ethnic background
- A lover, spouse, or parent
- One of your current teachers (grades can really get in the way of developing a mentoring relationship)
- Someone who holds grudges

How mentoring works:

- Either through a school program or on your own, find a mentor.
- Visit your mentor as often as you both agree to (such as biweekly or monthly).
- Develop a relationship to which you both contribute.

The mining operation: how to find your mentor

Actively seek out people who seem interested in you. Observe them. Think about the questions they ask, the advice they give, and how comfortable you feel in their presence.

You may have a mentor for a short or long period. Some mentors might know more about some academic areas than others. Some mentors may seem more like coaches: people who work with you on a very specific problem or skill, such as managing your time. Some mentors may be more oriented to discussing personal issues than others; and every mentor will have his own style.

Mentors won't meet your every need nor are they supposed to. But, with their support, you may be able to discover what else you need to do to stay motivated and meet your goals. Once you find your mentoring relationship, treasure it.

13.5 • How To Appreciate Your Work: Creating a Portfolio

College is packed with classes, assignments, tests, quizzes, projects, discussions, studying, friendships, and everyday living. It's virtually impossible to keep track of and appreciate all that you've learned. After the term is over, take a little time to celebrate your achievements. Try putting together an informal portfolio, which is actually a kind of scrapbook.

Assemble your portfolio:

- After the semester, scan your papers, homework, tests; school, internship, and service projects.
- As you sort through all these materials, you will become clearer about your criteria for selecting and excluding items for your portfolio.
- Try to select pieces that show both your most complete and best work as well as your earlier work. That way you'll have a better sense of how much you've grown.
- Select one or two items from each class (such as notes, papers, homework assignments, journal entries).
- Select or make mementos that represent extracurricular activities or times with friends.

Find out what you learned:

- What do your selections tell you are three to five of the most important things you learned this semester?
- At this point, what are your strongest areas? Your weakest? How do you know?
- What do you notice about yourself as a student?
- What do you notice about yourself as a friend?
- What did you contribute to your community?
- What do you notice about yourself as a thinker, reader, and writer?
- What do you need to remember for next semester or quarter?
- Who were you before the semester started? Who are you now?
- When you're done thinking about these questions, write or tape record your responses.

Make a good presentation:

- Find a good quality scrapbook, three-ring binder, or sturdy box that you label.
- If you're using a binder, look for acrylic page holders that can display and protect your work.
- Keep your portfolio package uncluttered and neat so that you can enjoy it.

Other ways to use your portfolio

Many instructors will ask you to keep a portfolio as a way of recording your progress and achievements. In both performance classes (graphic arts, illustrating, electronic music, etc.) and occupational classes (computer programming, teaching) portfolios will help you create a collection for future employers. In those cases, you will probably be displaying only your best work. Your portfolio's purpose(s) and audience(s) will have much influence on the selection and arrangement of your material. The care you take and the interesting effects you can create through your portfolio package can make a huge difference in how seriously your work is received.

Hey, *it's* Mr. Question-Person !

Each week Mr. Question-Person roams the campus armed with only a notebook and camera, seeking answers to today's hard student questions. He strikes without warning, so watch out: maybe this week you'll find yourself in Mr. Question-Person!

This week's question: How has creating a portfolio helped you?

Heda B.
Major: History

"When I looked back over everything I did this year, I was amazed at how far I've come. I didn't realize I could persist like I did. It was a battle but I won."

Ramon C.
Major: Counselling/Psych

"I didn't have much self-confidence, but my portfolio helped me acknowledge my hard work and accomplishments. Very theraputic!"

Nathan J.
Major: Computer Science

"I keep discovering new things I've learned. In fact, my current portfolio is Version 7.1!"

Amy G.
Major: Elementary Education

"I used to think I had nothing to say. But my papers and all show that I have a lot to say! Can I go now? I see somebody I need to talk to."

13.6 • Meet the Committee

We've all been there: You're beginning a project, getting ready for a date with some-one new, preparing to attempt something difficult, and suddenly there's a voice in your head, saying something like: "You can't do that paper!" or "That new person won't want to go out with you again!" or "Why do you even try that? You're going to look completely stupid." The voices in your head that speak up with criticism or negative messages just when you most need support or encouragement we call the Committee. Nobody really knows where the Committee comes from, but we all know where we'd like them to go.

Understanding the Committee:

- Perhaps the Committee echoes childhood messages.

- Perhaps the Committee is an overprotective part of yourself, trying to keep you at any cost from experiencing the pain of failure.

- Perhaps the Committee is giving you information about real fears that are holding you back.

- Perhaps you've created the Committee to give yourself an excuse for not taking risks.

When to get rid of the Committee:

- You start to feel like you can never do anything right.

- The messages keep you from doing things you really want to.

- You find you avoid beginning new projects or encounters.

- You're scared to turn in work because it's not "perfect."

- You're starting to develop a fear of failure—or a fear of success.

- Every time someone says something nice about you or your work, you feel compelled to point out all the things that are wrong about it—and you.

How to get rid of the Committee:

- Don't try to pretend that the message is not there. Listen carefully and then consciously tell yourself that you do not have to believe it.

- Picture the Committee as a group of people. Imagine them as amusing and ridicu-lous characters. Call them by name. Say: "Mabel, Fred, Esmerelda, get out of here!" Make sure that you see them as kind but misguided, not as omnipotent or evil.

- Believe that you have power over them: You do.

Believe it or not, there are times when it helps to keep the Committee around:

- Toward the end of a project, the Committee can nudge you into reviewing your work that final time, which might reveal some last-minute details to correct.

- Often, if there is something you could do better, such as a paragraph that you could improve by rewriting, the Committee will remind you of it.

- If you're experiencing some real doubt or hesitation about doing something that is, in fact, inappropriate or even dangerous, the Committee can raise a warning note and offer a kind of support that might allow you to say no.

The committee and perfectionism

It's useful and healthy to expect to do your best, hold yourself to high standards, and work hard to achieve them. However, some people think that means doing everything perfectly. Perfectionism is a trap because it doesn't allow you to grow, to learn from mistakes, to take risks, and ultimately to learn that "failure" can be a necessary part of success. The Committee represents a part of ourselves that has high–sometimes unrealistic– expectations. By knowing when to shoo them away and when to invite them back, you can begin to manage your own expectations in a way that can improve the quality of your work without wrecking the quality of your life.

13.7 • How To Be a Star in Your Own Show

Student life is dramatic, frequently melodramatic. Knowing this can help you step back a bit and become a star in your own show.

Benefits:

- By exaggerating your situation, you can understand it a little differently.
- It helps you anticipate what might go wrong so you can prepare yourself better.
- You get to laugh at yourself. (Better you than anyone else!)
- Laughter, even little snickers, breaks the tension.
- It beats whining or complaining about your situation.
- It's an inexpensive way to entertain yourself.

The Hollywood screen test: which role is *you*?

- You just completed the wrong assignment.
- You have twenty-three books to read this semester.
- You're getting a surprise quiz, and you're not up to date with the readings.
- You've been studying all night for an exam that's been canceled.
- You've just been exposed to the Hong Kong-Paraguayan-Hamintoshen flu.
- The dining room is serving Dreaded Veal Cutlet for the third day in a row.
- You have three classes that run back-to-back with no break.
- Your printer just broke down 30 minutes before your paper is due.
- An electrical storm has erased your work on the computer, and you have no hard-copy backup.
- Your child care arrangements aren't working out.
- The dog really ate your homework.

(Customize this list. If you can play the role, it's yours.)

Casting decisions:

- Any one of these: You're an extra.
- Any two of these: You're an understudy.
- Any three of these: You have a minor role with three to four lines.
- Any four of these: You're a supporting actor.
- Any five or more: You're the star!

Let's just say you have the perfect life with absolutely no trauma. (You're probably in denial, but we won't disturb that yet.) Congratulations!

You're ready to be a director in your friends' shows. Just apply the criteria above to their lives and, presto! You've got another show in the making.

The show casting can also be used for faculty! You just have to revise the criteria a bit. For example, instead of "You've completed the wrong assignment," for casting your professors' shows, you could substitute "You left the handout on the kitchen counter," "You lost the students' papers on the train," "You're boring yourself with your teaching style." Study your instructors: You're bound to find a star!

13.8 • Taking It on the Road!

It's like this: You've learned about lots of skills. When you count them up, you'll be amazed. And now, you have a choice: You can use these talents just until you've finished reading this book. Or you can keep using them every chance you get. Without practice, these tools will rust. With continuing practice you'll do better work and probably save yourself time and frustration.

So, turn "pro." Professionalize your skills by applying them whenever you're in a new situation or class. To help you, we've created this chart, which lists some of these abilities and their page references in this book. The final two columns are waiting for you to fill in: *where* (the specific class or situation) and *when* you're applying each skill. Now, take your show on the road: You're ready to be a star!

SKILL	PAGE	WHERE APPLIED	WHEN APPLIED
Brainstorming			
Mapping			
Previewing			
Making charts			
Notetaking			
Making marginal notes			
Saying no			
Speaking up in class			
Taking a stand			
Writing a journal			
Visualizing			
Revising			
Monitoring your own progress			
Planning your daily schedule			
Finding main points			
Summarizing			
Organizing your study area			
Participating in a study group			
Remembering information for tests			
Participating in class discussions			
Finding the ways you learn best			
Understanding an assignment			
Giving and receiving feedback			
Managing stress			

• *Activity 13.1*

Identify five successes you've had this week. Describe each success by naming it and telling what you did, said, or felt. Explain why each one is a success.

Name .... Date ....

• *Activity 13.2*

Look at the cartoon in "Meet the Committee". Draw or describe a one-panel cartoon about you and your own Committee. What are they saying to you and how does your character respond? If you'd like, try drawing the individual members of your Committee and giving them names.

Draw Yourself In

One of the best ways to enjoy and use this book is to create your own cartoon character. It's easy, and you don't need to know how to draw. That's right. You don't need to know how to draw!

The point is to create something that you can identify with, that will have a "voice" that expresses what you want to say in the way you choose to say it. Your character can interact with the other cartoon characters in the book in various situations or interact with other characters that you develop. Your character might be close to how you see yourself in your own life, or it might represent some other aspect of yourself, a way for you to act or speak that is normally difficult for you. Your character can be human, the same gender as you or not, an animal, or a unique construction of your own design. It's up to you.

Here's how to begin:

1. Take a deep breath, close your eyes, and relax.

2. Think about your own "ego"—your personality, how you express your needs and desires, and interact with the world—and ask yourself: "Does my ego look like something? Am I able to see it as a character? What kind of character would it be?"

3. Make a sketch of whatever comes to mind. If you're not a strong drawer, or if you think you can't draw at all, then just make a very simple sketch. Any kind of drawing will do: simple, complex, realistic, fantastic. Give yourself permission to draw what you like and like what you draw.

4. Give your character a name. This will probably change as you come to know your character better.

5. Think of an issue that is important to you. It might be something like saving the rainforest, helping the homeless, or reforming income tax law. Now, ask your character to make a comment about this issue. Look at your drawing and listen to what your character says. You'll be surprised how often your character will surprise you.

6. Write your character's words over his/her/its head, and draw a "bubble" (a circle with an arrow pointing to the character) around the words.

Congratulations! You've just created a simple cartoon.

If this exercise isn't working for you, keep trying. Another way is to think of a time when you wished you could have been more outspoken, more patient, or more some other way than you normally behave. Create a character who is that other "you", for example, the one who can speak eloquently when the real you is shy, the one who can be tactful when the real you is sometimes too blunt, the one who is frank when the real you is sometimes too "nice". See if you can find another voice through your character.

Like any sort of skill, this technique takes practice. Have fun as you begin to get to know your cartoon persona.

Appendix 2

Plan Your Own Weekly Schedule

	Monday	Tuesday	Wednesday	Thursday	Friday	Saturday	Sunday
6:00							
7:00							
8:00							
9:00							
10:00							
11:00							
12:00							
1:00							
2:00							
3:00							
4:00							
5:00							
6:00							
7:00							
8:00							
9:00							
10:00							

Appendix 3

Monthly Personal Budget Sheet

MONTHLY PERSONAL BUDGET SHEET

EXPENSES

Housing

rent/dorm/mortgage $_____

heat $_____

utilities $_____

insurance $_____

Transportation

car payment $_____

car insurance $_____

gas $_____

upkeep $_____

public transportation $_____

Food

groceries $_____

eating out/snacks $_____

Clothing $_____

Medical

insurance $_____

additional

doctors' bills $_____

prescriptions/over-the-counter meds $_____

School

tuition $_____

fees $_____

books $_____

supplies $_____

Entertainment $_____

Incidentals   (Xeroxing, gifts) $_____

Other $_____

TOTAL EXPENSES: $_____

INCOME

Job $_____

Loan $_____

Scholarships $_____

Other $_____

TOTAL INCOME: $_____

BALANCE

(positive or negative) $_____

Notes

Chapter 2

1. For the purposes of this chapter, we've summarized and adapted the first five of the seven stages of transition as described in Hopson, Barrie, and Mike Scally, *Transitions: Positive Change in Your Life & Work* (London: Pfeiffer & Company, 1993), pp. 17–27. The final two stages involve a search for the meaning of the transition within one's life and internalization of the transition.

2. For very nitty, gritty information on how to organize everything from closets to bills, see Eisenberg, Ronni with Kate Kelly, *Organize Yourself* (New York: MacMillan, 1986).

3. For motivational information on goal setting, read Zerafa, Judy, *Go For It!* (New York: Workman Publishing, 1982), Chapter 10. Also helpful information on goal setting in Davis, Martha. Elizabeth Robbins Eshelman, and Matthew McKay, *The Relaxation & Stress Reduction Workbook*, 4th ed. (Oakland, CA: New Harbinger Publications, Inc., 1995).

4. For an interesting fictional account of one student's college story, see the movie *Educating Rita*, available in most video rental stores.

Chapter 3

1. The Rehabilitation Act of 1973, Section 504 (Public Law 93112), states that "no otherwise qualified handicapped individual in the United States...shall, solely by reason of...handicap, be excluded from the participation in, be denied the benefits of, or be subjected to discrimination under any program or activity receiving Federal financial assistance." This legislation applies only to those in programs receiving federal financial assistance; since virtually all private postsecondary institutions receive federal funds (in such forms as Work Study money and research grants), nearly all postsecondary students with a disability are potentially covered under this legislation. The range of physical and mental conditions is vast and includes speech, visual, hearing impairments; cerebral palsy; epilepsy; muscular dystrophy; multiple sclerosis; cancer; diabetes; emotional illnesses; and specific learning disabilities, such as dyslexia and attention deficit disorder. The 1990 Americans with Disabilities Act (ADA) expands the protections offered under Section 504. An excellent resource that explains all this and more is *Testing Accommodations for Persons with Disabilities: A Guide for licensure, Certification and Credentialing*, authored by Warren L. King and Jane Jarrow and published by the Association on Higher Education and Disabilities, in Columbus, Ohio (614-488-4972). Another helpful booklet is *Section 504 of the Rehabilitation Act of 1973: The Rights of Individuals with Handicaps under Federal Law*, February 1989, published by the U.S. Department of Education, Office for Civil Rights, Washington D.C. 20202-1328.

2. For more information on visualization see Davis, Martha, Elizabeth Robbins Eshelman, and Matthew McKay, *The Relaxation & Stress Reduction Workbook*, 4th ed. (Oakland, CA: New Harbinger Publications, Inc., 1995).

3. Two books on Attention Deficit Disorder, both by Edward Hallowell, M.D. and John J. Ratey, M.D. are *Driven to Distraction* and *Answers to Distraction*. Both are published by Pantheon Books (New York) in 1994.

Chapter 4

1. More on procrastination in Mackenzie, Alec, *The Time Trap*. New York: AMACOM, 1990. The procrastination games are adapted from Ellis, Albert and William J. Knaus, *Overcoming Procrastination*. (New York: Signet 1977), pp. 97-108. James Sherman's *Stop Procrastinating* (Los Altos, CA: Crisp, 1989) identifies major causes of procrastination and makes helpful suggestions.

2. For other interesting ideas on time management, see Davidson, Jeff, *The Complete Idiot's Guide for Managing Your Time* (New York: Alpha/MacMillan, 1995).

Chapter 5

1. Summary length, as suggested by Charles Bazerman, *The Informed Writer*, 4th ed. (Boston: Houghton Mifflin Company, 1991), p. 92 is about one-quarter of the original passage. Bazerman has an excellent discussion on a variety of ways to create effective summaries in Chapter four. One of the best discussions anywhere on using the margins is also in Bazerman's text, pp. 19-23.

2. We recommend Fulwiler, Toby, ed., *The Journal Book* (Portsmouth, NH: Boynton, Cook, 1987), for a fuller discussion on the use of journals within many kinds of classes.

3. For more on notetaking, see Fry, Ron, *Take Notes*, 2nd ed. (Hawthorne, NJ: Career Press, 1994).

Chapter 6

1. One of the best books on writing as a process is still Peter *Elbow's Writing Without Teachers*: (New York: Oxford University Press, 1973). Elbow also includes many tips for giving and receiving feedback. Another text that includes information on feedback is Elbow, Peter and Pat Belanoff, *Sharing and Responding*. New York: Random House, 1989).

2. Axelrod, Rise B. and Charles R. Cooper, *The St. Martin's Guide to Writing*, short 3rd ed. (New York: St. Martin's Press, 1991) includes an excellent discussion on many ways of getting started. Some of the ideas from 6.4 are adapted from this text.

Chapter 7

1. Sharyn was part of a study group for two years when she was preparing for her doctoral comprehensive exams and writing her dissertation. Participating in this four-person group, which usually met biweekly, made the whole process of getting a doctorate much more manageable and exciting. Sharyn has also been part of a number of fiction writers' groups. Peaco, too, has participated in several groups for both fiction and non-fiction writing. Both Sharyn and Peaco have used a variety of student writing groups in their courses.

Chapter 8

1. Additional test taking strategies in Silver, Theodore, J.D., *The Princeton Review Study Smart* (New York: Villard, 1994).

Chapter 9

1. For more on notetaking in class, see Fry, Ron, *Take Notes*, 2nd ed. (Hawthorne, NJ: Career Press, 1994).

2. When you think about protesting, or even just discussing a grade, realize that you might be entering into a situation that is a form of negotiation, a subject that has gotten a lot of attention. For more on negotiation, see Fisher, Roger, William Ury, and Bruce Patton, *Getting to Yes*, 2nd ed. (New York: Penguin Books, 1991).

Chapter 10

1. For more on criticism, see Hathaway, Patti, *Giving and Receiving Criticism: Your Key to Interpersonal Success* (Menlo Park, CA: Crisp Publications, Inc., 1990).

2. For discussion on interpersonal styles on managing disagreements and other suggestions for making requests and responding to feedback, we recommend Davis, Martha, Elizabeth Robbins Eshelman, and Matthew McKay, *The Relaxation & Stress Reduction Workbook*, 4th ed. (Oakland, CA: New Harbinger Press, 1995), pp. 187-209.

3. There are many books on the subject of conflict resolution, including *Talk It Out: Conflict Resolution in the Elementary Classroom* by Barbara Porro, ASCD Books, which Peaco illustrated. Some schools even have peer mediation opportunities in which trained students help to mediate disputes.

Chapter 12

1. An extremely helpful reference to visualization, breathing, meditation, and other stress reduction methods is Davis, Martha, Elizabeth Robbins Eshelman, and Matthew McKay, *The Relaxation & Stress Reduction Workbook*, 4th ed. (Oakland, CA: New Harbinger Publications, Inc. 1995).

References

Axelrod, Rise B. and Charles R. Cooper, *The St. Martin's Guide to Writing*, short 3rd ed. New York, New York, St. Martin's Press, 1991.

Bazerman, Charles, *The Informed Writer*, 4th ed. Boston, Massachusetts: Houghton Mifflin Company, 1991.

Davidson, Jeff, *The Complete Idiot's Guide for Managing Your Time*. New York, New York: Alpha/MacMillan, 1995.

Davis, Martha, Elizabeth Robbins Eshelman, and Matthew McKay, *The Relaxation & Stress Reduction Workbook*, 4th ed. Oakland, CA: New Harbinger Publications, Inc., 1995.

Eisenberg Ronni with Kate Kelly, *Organize Yourself*. New York, New York: MacMillan, 1986.

Elbow, Peter, *Writing Without Teachers*. New York, New York: Oxford University Press, 1973.

Elbow, Peter and Pat Belanoff, *Sharing and Responding*. New York, New York: Random House, 1989.

Ellis, Albert and William J. Knaus, *Overcoming Procrastination*. New York, New York: Signet, 1977.

Fisher, Roger, William Ury, and Bruce Patton, *Getting to Yes*, 2nd ed. New York, New York: Penguin Books, 1991.

Fry, Ron, *Take Notes*, 2nd ed. Hawthorne, NJ: Career Press, 1994.

Fulwiler, Toby, editor, *The Journal Book*. Portsmouth, NH: Boynton Cook, 1987.

Hallowell, Edward and John Ratey, *Answers to Distraction*. New York, New York: Pantheon Books, 1994.

---, *Driven to Distraction*. New York, New York: Pantheon Books, 1994.

Hathaway, Patti, *Giving and Receiving Criticism: Your Key to Interpersonal Success.* Menlo Park, CA: Crisp Publications, Inc., 1990.

Hopson, Barrie and Mike Scally, *Transitions: Positive Change in Your Life & Work.* London, England: Pfeiffer & Company, 1993.

King, Warren L. and Jane Jarrow, *Testing Accommodations for Persons with Disabilities: A Guide for Licensure, Certification and Credentialing.* Columbus, OH: Association on Higher Education and Disabilities, 1993.

Mackenzie, Alec, *The Time Trap.* New York, New York: AMACOM, 1990.

Sherman, James. *Stop Procrastinating.* Los Altos, CA: Crisp Publications, 1989.

Silver, Theodore, J.D., *The Princeton Review Study Smart.* New York, New York: Villard, 1994.

U.S. Department of Education, Office for Civil Rights, *Section 504 of the Rehabilitation Act of 1973: The Rights of Individuals with Handicaps under Federal Law.* Washington, D.C., 1989.

Zerafa, Judy, *Go for It!* New York, New York: Workman Publishing, 1982.

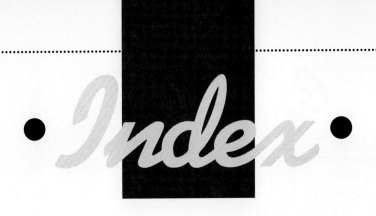

Index

Calendar, 56-57
Canceling appointments/commitments, 240-41
Cartoon characters:
    creating your own, 271-74
    Meet the Cast, 1-6
    See cartoons throughout the text
Challenges, learning, 28-29
Charts, creating/understanding, 106-7
Cheating, 196-99
    defined, 196
    penalties for, 197
    reasons to avoid, 198
Class attendance, and professors, 190-91
Class discussions, participating in, 184-85
Classroom style, professors, 180-81
Closing paragraphs, 124
Clothing, for tests/quizzes, 170
College:
    longing for life before, 210
    reasons for attending, 8-9
College campus, surveying, 5
Color codes, 80
Commitments, negotiating your way out of, 240-41
Committee, The:
    meeting, 262-63
    and perfectionism, 263
Communication, 18
    and international students, 44
Comparison shopping, for credit cards, 218
Concentration, 36-37
Contingency planning, 80
Control, loss of, 244-45
Conversation partner, with international student, 46
Conversation starters, for disagreements, 206
Creative present giving, 220
Creativity, unleashing, 121

Credit cards, 218-19
    comparison shopping, 218
    debt load, managing, 219
    interest rate, 218
    taking care of, 218-19
Criticism, handling, 208-9
Critiquing, 134

Daily plan, 56-57
    fine-tuning, 56
Daily priority schedule, 58
Daily rhythms, 32-33
Debt load, managing, 219
Delivery style, professors', 181
Department secretaries, befriending, 13
Disabilities, 30-31
    accommodations, 30
    documentation papers, 30
    sharing information about, 30
    students' responsibility, 31
    testing/work adjustments for, 30-31
Disagreements with others, 206-7
Documentation papers, to verify disabilities, 30
Drafts, 126-27
Drop-in visitor, managing, 68

$\mathcal{E}$

Earphones/ear plugs, and noise interference, 34-35
Effective writing, 111-42
    See also Writing
End of class, professors' signal for, 181
Equipment, library, 40
Essay questions, preparing for, 164-65
    See also Tests
Essays, writing, and knowledge of audience, 123
    See also Writing

Essay tests, 168–69
Exam fever, 172–73
Example projects, 144
Explaining, as way of saying no, 204
Extracurricular activities, 46–47

Faculty feedback, using, 186–87
Faculty lectures/presentations, listening
    to, 182–83
    See also Professors
Feedback:
    asking for/listening to, in writing
        groups, 134–35
    faculty, using, 186–87
    giving, 134–35
Final drafts, 126–27
Final exam, 172–76
    compared to other tests, 172
    studying for, 172
"Finding" money, 224–25
First paragraph, 124
First week activities, 12–13
Fitting all the pieces together, 18–19
Fonts, 130
Font variations, 130
Foreign student advisor, 44
Freebies, checking out, 220
Freewriting, 118
Frustration, See Stress management

Goal setting, 16–16
Gourmet study session, 62–63
Grades:
    discussing/protesting, 192–93
    taking personally, 193
Graphic design techniques,
    130–31

Grogginess, and lateness, 66
Group sessions, running, 154–55

Hard times, 229–50
    breakup of a relationship,
        238–39
    feeling lousy, 236–37
    giving up, avoiding, 246–47
    hot seat, negotiating your way out
        of, 240–41
    loss of control, 244–45
    making a big mistake, 242–43
    See also Stress
Heads, 130
Hedging, as way of saying no, 204
Hidden time, finding, 78–79
Hollywood screen test, 264
Homesickness, 210
Homework, and lateness, 66
Hot seat, negotiating your way out of,
    240–41
Humor, using, as way of saying no,
    204
    See also cartoons throughout the
        text
Hunt for clothing, and lateness, 66

Impulse buying, 221
Increasing your income, strategies for,
    222–23
Insufficient information, and
    revisions, 128–29
Interest rate, credit cards, 218
International students, 44–45
Interruptions, 68–69

organization options, 98
personal reading journal:
    assigning, 103
    keeping, 102-3
reviewing your notes, 98
when to take notes, 98

Opening paragraphs, 124
Organization:
    strategies for, 148-49
    in writing, 124-25
Organizing notes, 98
Orientation, 12-13
Outline, 118
Overlooked achievements, examples
    of, 254
Oversleeping, and lateness, 66

Peers, disagreeing with, 206
Penalties for cheating/plagiarism,
    197
Perfectionism, and The Committee,
    263
Personal information, sharing with
    professors, 189
Personal reading journal:
    assigning, 103
    how to use, 103
    keeping, 102-3
Personal reasons, for attending
    college, 8
Plagiarism, 196-99
    avoiding, 196
    defined, 196
    penalties for, 197
    reasons to avoid, 198
Point size, fonts, 130
Portable student, reinventing yourself,
    252-53

Portfolio, creating, 260-61
Power reading, 85-97
    See also Readers; Reading
Present giving, creative, 220
Prioritizing, 58-59
Procrastination, 74-77
    excuses, 74
    games, 76
    overcoming, 74-77
Professors, 177-200
    assignment style, 181
    beginning of class, 180
    cheating/plagiarism, 196-99
    and class attendance, 190-91
    classroom style, assessing,
        180-81
    delivery style, 181
    discussing/protesting grades,
        192-93
    end of class, signal for, 181
    faculty feedback, using, 186-87
    faculty lectures/presentations,
        listening to, 182-83
    meeting outside class, 188-89
    organization, 180
    reading expectations, 181
    sexual harassment, 195
    sharing personal information with,
        189
    signal of what's important, 180
    syllabus, 178-79
    uncomfortable feelings with,
        194-95
Project cycles, understanding,
    150-51
Project management:
    keeping track, 148
    project cycles, 150-51
    scheduling for, 146
Protesting grades, 192-93

Questions, asking when reading,
    94-95
Quizzes, *See* Tests/quizzes

R

Readers:
  benefits to, 86
  qualifications of, 86
  responsibilities of, 86
Reading, 85-97
  identifying purpose for, 88
  main points, finding, 92-93
  questions, asking, 94-95
  summarizing, 96-97, 106
  tutoring, 38
  why you should care about, 87
Reading assignment:
  beginning, 90-91
  getting a grip on, 90
  how much to study for, 60
  orientation, 90
Reading comprehension, as learning
    challenge, 29
Reading expectations, of professors, 181
Reading journal:
  assigning, 103
  how to use, 103
  keeping, 102-3
Reading pronunciation, as learning
    challenge, 29
Reasons for attending college, 8-9
Reference librarians, 40
Relationship breakup, 238-39
Research sources, 40-41
  evaluating, 40
  library, 40
Reviewing notes, 98
Revisions, 128-29
Rewards, 256-57
Rough drafts, 126-27

S

Sample papers, using, 136-37
Sans serif fonts, 130
Saying no, 204-5
Schedules, gathering support for, 64-65

Scheduling:
  assignments, 146-47
  for the semester, 54-55
Seating, for tests/quizzes, 170
Self-blame, and revisions, 128-29
Self-esteem, and transitions, 11
Self-exile, and revisions, 129
Serif fonts, 130
Session format, study group, 154
Sexual harassment, 195
Short-answer questions, 162-63
  tips for, 166-67
Signs, and interruptions, 69
Skills, professionalizing, 266-67
Small groups, participating in, 184-85
Small project, anatomy of, 146
Social reasons, for attending college, 4
Social timing, as learning challenge,
    29
Spatial orientation, as learning
    challenge, 29
Special events, library, 40
Special spaces, library, 40
Spellchecking, 116
Strengths:
  discovering, 24-25
  growing from weaknesses, 25
Strengths journal, 51
Stress/stress management, 230-35
  break up of relationship, 238
  and losing things, 72-73
  mental balance, restoring, 234
  negotiating out of hot seat, 240
  planning/implementing strategies,
    234
  responding to, 232-33
  stressful situations, 230
    making list of, 231
  support/information, seeking, 234
Stretching limited resources, 220-21
Student life:
  casting decisions, 264
  Hollywood screen test, 264
  starring in your own show, 264-65
  taking it on the road, 266-70
Student papers:
  obtaining, 136
  personal reactions to, applying, 137
  working with, 136-37

T

U

V

Visualization, 48-52
  scenario, 48
  of successful testing, 170
  tips about, 48
Voice mail/e-mail messages, 68

W

Weekly schedule, 56-57
  planning, 275-77
White noise gadgets, and noise inter-
    ference, 34
White space, 130
Work-related trips/events, and missed
    time from class, 18
Work schedule vs. class schedule, 18
Writer's block, 132-33
Writing, 111-42
  audience, 122
  brainstorming, 120-21
  bullets, 130
  choices, 112
  closing paragraphs, 124
  dancing/singing interpretation of
      assignment, 119
  details in, 116
  drafts, 126-27
  finishing, 116
  fonts, 130
  font variations, 130
  forms of, 112

freewriting, 118
graphic design techniques, 130-31
as hard work, 112
heads, 130
how to think about, 112-13
introduction, 116
as learning challenge, 29
myths about, 114-15
opening paragraphs, 124
organization, 124-25
outline/mapping, 118
as a process, 116-17
questions:
    about writing, 118
    before turning in paper, 138
    in early writing stages, 138
revisions, 128-29
rough and final drafts, 126-27
sample papers, 136-37
spellchecking, 116
starting, 116, 118-19
subheads, 130
sudden insight, 119
talking to others/yourself, 118
topics, listing/selecting, 118
tutoring, 38
white space, 130
as work in progress, 112
writer's block, 132-33
writing groups, 134-35
Writing assignments, how much to
    study for, 60
Writing groups, 134-35
  asking for/listening to feedback,
      134-35
  creating, 135
  critiquing, 134
  sample scenario, 134